To Fred,
for helping me find
Jesus again

And to my mother, Judy,
who introduced me to him
in the first place

SAFFRON CROSS

THE UNLIKELY STORY OF HOW A CHRISTIAN MINISTER MARRIED A HINDU MONK

J. DANA TRENT

FRESH AIR BOOKS®

The Fresh Air Books website http://books.upperroom.org/fresh-air-books/

Fresh Air Books® is an imprint of Upper Room Books®. Fresh Air Books® and design logos are trademarks owned by The Upper Room®, a ministry of GBOD®, Nashville, Tennessee. All rights reserved.

Cover photo: Franklin Golden
Cover and interior design: Marc Whitaker / www.mtwdesign.net
Typesetting: PerfecType, Nashville, TN

Library of Congress Cataloging-in-Publication Data
Trent, J. Dana.
 Saffron cross : the unlikely story of how a Christian minister married a Hindu monk / by J. Dana Trent.
   pages cm
 ISBN 978-1-935205-16-6 (print)—ISBN 978-1-935205-17-3 (mobi)—ISBN 978-1-935205-18-0 (epub)
1. Trent, J. Dana. 2. Baptists—Clergy—Biography. 3. Interfaith marriage. 4. Christianity and other religions—Hinduism. 5. Hinduism—Relations—Christianity. 6. Marriage—Religious aspects--Hinduism. 7. Marriage—Religious aspects—Christianity. 8. Chaitanya (Sect) I. Title.
 BX6495.T674A3 2013
 286'.1092—dc23
 [B]   2013024362
Printed in the United States of America

CONTENTS

ACKNOWLEDGMENTS

I could fill all the pages of this book with names of individuals who have touched my life in some major or minor fashion, but that would keep you from getting to the story, and you'd resent me.

This book could not have been written without Fred, who lived these pages, groaned through each awkward sentence, and remained steadfast during many emotional months. He is my rock, editor, and self-proclaimed life coach. I'll let him keep that last title because being a writer's spouse is an arduous task. He pushed laughter to the forefront at every turn, and for that he deserves a gold medal or, at the very least, liberation from reincarnation.

I am first a daughter, sister, granddaughter, aunt, niece, and cousin to the best family in the universe. Thank you, Joines, Trents, Lewmans, and Eakers. You have been remarkable from the start, especially my brother, Dr. Ron Joines, whose appetite for life is contagious.

Special thanks to the Upper Room Books team for taking a chance on a Southern Baptist minister who married a Hindu monk. I am especially grateful for Jeannie Crawford-Lee, Joanna Bradley, Lauren Hirsch, Whitney Booth, Anne Trudel, Pamela McClure, and Janice Neely, who were excited and endlessly patient with my questions and anxieties.

Thanks to the world's best friends, who offered a steady stream of motivational speeches: Britainy Lewman Sholl, Erin Lewman Riggs, Kate Amos Harris, the Rev. Carol D. Estes, Kristin Beran Krupp, the Rev. Jennifer Allen Hege, and Madeline Chenoweth Day.

Dr. Mary Caler and Judy W. Trent tolerated the very first terrible draft, as only a dear friend and mother would do.

Where would I be without the faith communities who nurtured my spirituality over three decades and built this book without even knowing it? Thank you to the members and ministers of Olin T. Binkley Memorial Baptist Church, First Baptist Church Reidsville, and the Dana Community Bible Church. Special thanks to the academic and professional communities who also offered their care: Salem College, Duke Divinity School, and the UNC Health Care Department of Pastoral Care.

Boundless thanks to Swami B. V. Tripurari and the Gaudiya Vaishnava communities of Saragrahi and Audarya, who lovingly opened their arms and hearts to a Christian minister.

Long before there was a book, there were dreams of a book. Many creative and professional mentors tolerated my grandiosity and shaped me as an artist: Lauren F. Winner, John Utz, Enuma Okoro, Jason Byassee, Sherry Williamson, Jonathan Goldstein, Elisabeth Stagg, Rev. Dr. Jo Bailey Wells, Rev. Sally G. Bates, Dr. Ellen F. Davis, Dr. Curtis Freeman, Rev. Liz Dowling-Sendor, and Dr. Robert Seymour. Before these heroes, there were patient teachers who saw a budding—if not messy and untamed—calling: Tim Poe, Margaret Apple, Joan Kimmel, Starr McHugh, Mary Ellen Guzy, and Penelope Niven.

Thanks to the Art Institute of Raleigh-Durham for its flexibility in my teaching schedule this year. I'm also grateful to Organizational Solutions (OS Inc.) and the PTA Thrift Shop Executive Team, whose members were constant cheerleaders while I balanced my day job and book writing.

Last but not least, there are those who have gone on before me, saving seats near the chocolate fountain and box of cuddly kittens: Evelyn Wade Trent, Charles Trent, Dorothy and Richard Lewman, Richard J. Lewman Jr. (The King), Ann Trent McAlister, and Phyllis Hopkins Morningstar. I carry you with me each day.

CHAPTER

SEX-FREE HONEYMOON

From one human being [God] created all races of people and made them live throughout the whole earth. [God] fixed beforehand the exact times and the limits of the places where they would live. [God] did this so that they would look for [the Divine]. . . . Yet God is actually not far from any one of us.

Adapted from Acts 17:26-27, GNT

I didn't have sex on my honeymoon. Instead, I spent two weeks as a religious minority in the small village of Vrindavan among fifty-seven thousand Hindus to commemorate the Christian-Hindu interfaith marriage between me, the Baptist minister, and Fred, the Western-born former Hindu monk.

Fred and I arrived in New Delhi after midnight three days before Christmas and five months after our July nuptials. In the two years I had known him, he incessantly warned me that India would be an assault on my senses, but I hadn't prepared myself for the truth of his counsel. As we exited the airport, the automatic doors opened to reveal a dusty city that smelled as if every resident had lit a match and ceremoniously blown it out at the same time. The sulfur-infused darkness foreshadowed a daylight reality: India didn't smell or look like paradise.

From the airport, Fred and I traveled forty minutes with our driver, Deepak, through the smog, dodging bedraggled delivery trucks and enduring horns until we reached a three-story building. The online advertisement for the hotel boasted "Western-style" accommodations, and by Indian standards, it was the Waldorf Astoria. But by American standards, it was the shady roadside motel that most of us avoided.

In the lobby of the hotel Fred and I met the young Indian men who worked there, slept there, ate what food their guests left behind, and washed and hung their only pair of pants and shirt out to dry on the filthy rooftop. Less than an hour in, I'd already slammed face-first into the socioeconomic and culture shock of Indian society.

Fred and I boarded a narrow elevator and arrived at the threshold of room 217. The men waited for our approval. Fred nodded that, yes, the room was fine. They exhaled, relieved. Once they were out of sight, Fred turned to me to offer his usual, thoughtful check-in.

"How are you, my sweet?"

I said nothing and collapsed in his arms. We had been married fewer than six months, and Fred was saintly in his patience for my anxieties. His monastic training served him well; his intuitive, sensitive nature quieted my sharp, spoiled edges.

I accepted his directions to get in the shower, which was really just a stall holding a plastic red pail. One hour and one hot water bucket bath later, I was sound asleep and had forgotten we were seven thousand miles from home. I remembered only once I woke up to what sounded like a Jewish shofar on Rosh Hashanah* and Fred smiling on the edge of the bed as he watched flamboyant Bollywood music videos on the small color TV. It was 4:45 a.m.; we were in India. I groaned and pulled the covers over my head. The four-hour journey to Vrindavan and a sex-free honeymoon still awaited us.

On the hotel's carefully partitioned rooftop, we ate a hearty breakfast of *parathas*, fried unleavened bread infused with potatoes or vegetables.

---

*I later learned that Hindus have a similar worship ritual using a conch shell.

Heavy fabric divided the space to protect Westerners from unsightly urban clotheslines, trash, and clutter. I peeked past the curtain to get my first glimpse of New Delhi in the daylight, which served only to confirm my midnight suspicions. Dingy clothes hung from sagging lines, rooftop nooks held heaps of litter, and wild dogs on the street below sniffed piles of rubble.

"Where are we?" I wondered aloud.

India's landscape was unlike any poverty-stricken American city I'd ever seen. Helplessness turned my *paratha*-filled belly into knots of guilt as Fred and I were shuffled downstairs to wait for a small sedan with no shocks and hard seats to take us to the holy village of Vrindavan. Guilt turned to panic when we got in the car and I discovered that placing yourself (willingly or otherwise) in a moving vehicle in India means increasing your chances of getting smashed by an oxen-powered wagon hauling an unrestrained load of handmade bricks by about ten thousand percent. This doesn't include the other elevated risks of colliding with a motorcycle carrying three adults and an infant, rickshaw drivers, farm animals, and pedestrians. Indian travel is full of near misses.

The traffic leaving New Delhi was chaotic and terrifying. There were no rules, stoplights, stop signs, yielding, lanes, or crosswalks. Cars, trucks, bicycles, rickshaws, motorcycles, wagons, and school children fought for the right-of-way. There were no child-safety seats or seat belts in India. Small children rode loosely on the backs of ill-guided scooters, making American air bags and antilock brakes look overly cautious. Rainbow swirls of brightly colored cloth danced through the haze as travelers raced to their destinations. Vehicles were painted colorfully with the words *Horn Please!*—a plea for drivers to sound their horns whenever near another vehicle—but this only created a deafening cacophony.

Fred stoically hugged the car window and videotaped the ordeal while I prayed. "Holy Mary, Mother of God," I whispered, "pray for us sinners now and in the hour of our death—which I am certain is imminent." I added the last part for good measure.

Vrindavan, our interfaith honeymoon destination, was nestled ninety-four miles from New Delhi's hustle and bustle. It took four hours to travel there with just one roadside stop, a rest area congested with beggars clutching tutu-wearing monkeys who offered circus tricks in exchange for money.

Our New Delhi driver warned us in broken English not to talk to monkey handlers and to keep the car windows rolled up. Fred and I exchanged looks, imagining he was exaggerating. But once the driver was out of sight, a beggar brought his ballerina monkey to hang onto my window and scream for money. When that didn't work, he offered to snap a photo of us with the creature—a classic tourist scam to steal cameras.

I was relieved to return to the road. Traffic subsided through India's countryside, and we arrived in the village of Vrindavan. If New Delhi smelled like chaos, Vrindavan smelled like divinity. The main road leading to town showcased colorful billboards depicting the construction of luxury apartments for New Delhi refugees longing for spiritual sanity. As prominent as the plastic Lord Ganesha glued to our driver's dashboard, Vrindavan's vibe was sacred and renewing—a space in which we remember who we are and whose we are.

The puttering sedan inched along, and we passed a nearly four-story statue of Hanuman the Protector—who is half-monkey, half-man—and many lavish temples. This village wore its religion on its sleeve—and that religion was not Christianity. God was not hidden away in steepled spaces for Sunday adoration; instead, the Eastern God exploded onto the scene—touching all animate and inanimate objects with gilded glory. Non-Protestant symbols of God adorned automobiles, street vendors, shacks, and businesses. From the dirty window of an Indian man's car, I realized for the first time in my life that I was in the religious minority.

Still, I didn't make a distinction between the Eastern God I was witnessing and my own Western God. The entire village exuded sacred mysteries and worship. God was at the center of life, not on the periphery. This town was unabashedly proud of its religious affiliation; it made no apologies or efforts to conceal its identity as a holy place—and that invigorated me. The landscape dripped with spirituality, and I became a spectator of this miracle and a recipient of its grace. Here I learned interfaith marriage lesson number one: God is god, east or west, and is too precious to ignore.

But how *does* a born-and-raised Southern Baptist, who at age twelve could recite all of the books of the Bible in order, end up in the backseat of an Indian man's car in a village of fifty-seven thousand devout Hindus?

It happened because I fell in love with a former Hindu monk who had given me everything in just the two short years I'd know him. He was a mirror to my soul—and the adventure was just beginning.

I looked to Fred, who was lovingly taking in my reaction to this foreign place. He gave my hand a knowing squeeze. Shortly after we had begun dating, Fred shared the personal significance Vrindavan held for him as the homeland of Lord Krishna, the cowherd boy who, according to the Gaudiya Vaishnava sect of Hinduism, is the Supreme Personality of God. Vrindavan is to Gaudiya Vaishnavas what Bethlehem is to Christians and Mecca is to Muslims: the auspicious birthplace of the Divine. Fred spent his twenty-fifth birthday in Vrindavan as a monk, just months before his journey to Audarya Monastery to serve and study with his *guru*.

I glanced around at the Indians walking the streets with sacred clay markings on their foreheads, *japa* prayer beads in cloth bags dangling from their necks. Their loud religious greetings melded into a divine hum, and I knew this sex-free honeymoon would change me forever.

India was a testimony to our Christian-Hindu interfaith marriage—a means of solidifying our commitment to God and our east-meets-west path. Fred had so lovingly agreed to be married in my Baptist church and always found himself surrounded by Christian practices in the Bible Belt of North Carolina. This honeymoon provided an opportunity for the two of us to experience Fred's world of prayer, worship, and spirituality. I hadn't realized how much it would affect me.

When Fred and I first discussed honeymoons, I wanted the quintessential tropical getaway that I felt was my due. I was twenty-nine and the perpetual bridesmaid who had endured a decade of friends' rice-filled farewells to romantic destinations. But Fred had begged me to go to India since I met him. I didn't understand the appeal; it seemed risky, dirty, and not at all relaxing.

"Yes," Fred would say, "it's all of those things—and so much more."

I was beginning to understand the *so much more*.

Fred wanted me to immerse myself in the cultural context that birthed his religious practices. He wanted me to understand why he chose the path of Hinduism, and to do that we had to get to the root of it. I was resentful. I whined. I visited the State Department's web site on travel safety and crafted elaborate presentations in my mind on all the possible catastrophic scenarios and dangers of an Indian ashram honeymoon.

Fred didn't feed into my drama, which is his tried-and-true method of loving me. Instead, he listened patiently because he knew that visiting Vrindavan was essential to forging our Christian-Hindu path. Seven thousand miles, twelve hours of Indian culture shock, and one monkey in a tutu later, I realized he had been right. Melding two religions into a single spiritual household would keep us together, but the unknown by-product would be my refreshed, strengthened Christian faith.

Vrindavan's serenity buried New Delhi's commotion, and it became obvious why we chose this honeymoon in lieu of sandy beaches and oceanfront daiquiris. We arrived at Mayapura Vrindavan Trust (MVT), a renowned Vrindavan ashram and temple complex built by His Divine Grace A. C. Bhaktivedanta Swami Prabhupada, the monk responsible for bringing the Gaudiya Vaishnavism tradition of Hinduism to America in the 1960s.

MVT is a gated community and haven for international practitioners of Gaudiya Vaishnavism. Iron doors, stoic guards, and territorial street dogs protect visitors from the reality of India's hectic streets and tourism vulnerabilities. Outside the gate is a side street of conveniences for captive Westerners: a corner store, Internet café, international telephone services, and money exchangers. When business was slow, bored shopkeepers gathered in the street to taunt rooftop monkeys with green apples. Inside the MVT gates, no such funny business was allowed. The property emanated reverence—neither monkey nor human misbehavior were tolerated.

An ashram is a Hindu temple, monastery, and residential community that typically accommodates religious pilgrims. There are also permanent ashram residents—the monks who care for the temple and its deities and the administrative staff who tend the facilities. Just as it was popularized in the memoir *Eat, Pray, Love*, an ashram is a place of religious study, spiritual practice, meditation, worship, and respite. Ashrams vary in shape, size, and seriousness. MVT ashram is large and purposeful—pilgrims come to worship Lord Krishna, and strict rules help keep the community intentional and focused.

Fred visited MVT on his previous Indian pilgrimage. He was familiar with its safe and quiet life inside the gates. Fred knew my anxieties well enough to know that MVT would be just my speed—cloistered, safe, and calming. MVT was clean and quaint with its gardens (green even in December), simple rooms, and frequent electrical outages (endearing after a while). Our room had two twin beds—not ideal for honeymooning—that we pushed together like giddy lovers, even though, per ashram rules, there was no sex to be had. A large, serious-looking portrait of temple founder Srila Prabhupada hung on the wall opposite the twin beds to ensure that honeymooners and other guests obeyed this tenet.

Months earlier, Fred and I had discussed the implications of a sex-free honeymoon while booking flights.

"You think we'll be tempted?" I asked, fairly certain that I would be.

"Nah. The last thing India makes you feel is sexy."

Fred was right. The first twenty-four hours in India had only made me feel dusty.

The ashram guest room floors were speckled like elementary school classroom tiles, and the wooden door to our room was secured only with a padlock. Each room held a small desk with a copy of the *Bhagavad Gita* (Hindu scripture), just like Gideon Bibles that reside in American hotel nightstands. A hot water heater was mounted on the bathroom wall and could be switched on fifteen minutes before a desired bath time. The heater guaranteed five minutes of a steady stream of hot water or a large red plastic bucket full, whichever was preferred or tolerated on chilly December mornings.

The MVT bathroom had a Western toilet with porcelain foot grippers for balance—in case you wanted to do your business Eastern style (standing with your feet flat on the sides of the toilet seat and squatting—an act that required very careful coordination). Fred practiced this move on our apartment toilet and could execute it perfectly. I, however, am completely inept at squats and quickly become the laughingstock of personal trainers and aerobics classes.

The east-meets-west toilet seemed tolerable, but I was horrified when I sat to pee Western style, reached for the paper, and noticed the absence of a roll. Fred had warned me of the assault on my senses, but he had neglected the minor detail that Indians don't wipe with paper.

"Freeeeeeed," I hollered in my North Carolinian drawl.

15

"Yes, my sweet?"

"There's no toilet paper," I grumbled, pants around my ankles, in quite a precarious position.

Fred offered a "this is going to be a long trip" sigh and pointed to the little bowl on the floor, which Indians typically use in lieu of paper. This apparatus is used to rinse while the left hand is used to wipe*. While this system may be environmentally friendly, I'm not sure how well it fares in the disease prevention category.

Panic ensued. I'm an avid toilet paper fan, and I had brought only two travel packs of tissues, which Fred retrieved. I knew they wouldn't last me long. Still sitting on the toilet, I self-soothed my way through the cultural sensitivity and courage I was going to need to make this interfaith marriage and honeymoon work. It was important to show Fred that I was not an American princess who couldn't adapt. I wanted him to feel assured that he had made a wise decision in choosing me. I closed my eyes and prayed for toilet paper.

A solution arrived after hours of anxiety while Fred and I ate at the ashram's vegetarian restaurant. I noticed a stack of napkins adjacent to the cash register for takeout orders. With Handel's "Hallelujah Chorus" ringing, I saw my opportunity. I took a few and discreetly placed them in my pocket as we exited the restaurant. I was a thief in the Lord's house, but I had toilet paper for the night.

I repeated this process each day during the first week of our stay. I felt terrible for stealing paper napkins from a temple, so I finally mustered the courage to ask the front desk attendant if there was any toilet paper in the entire village.

The attendant pointed me to a corner convenience store that, embarrassingly enough, had been there all along outside of MVT gates. I walked to the shop and sheepishly asked the shop owner for a roll of toilet paper. He snickered; I was a pitiful white girl standing in his establishment begging for toilet paper because I was too much of a coward to use my own

---

*In India, one's left hand is used only for bathroom business, while the right hand is dominant for everything else (for example eating, worship, and business transactions). This works swimmingly for everyone—except the left-handers—who are subject to stares and scolding if caught not obeying this cultural and religious norm. I am left-handed.

hand. I'd been defeated by India's prehistoric sanitation system, and I was looking to him to save me.

The shop owner grumbled, "Eighty rupees!" while holding back a belly laugh. I slapped the equivalent of two US dollars in rupees on his counter, tucked my purchase under my shirt, and dashed back to the ashram, relieved.

That first afternoon, after settling into our room, Fred decided we should make our inaugural visit to the Krishna-Balarama Temple adjacent to the MVT residential complex. The temple was large and sprawling, running the length of Vrindavan's main street and separated by a tall wall to shut out the road filled with beggars, pedestrians, and street vendors. The temple catered to New Delhians, Westerners, and religious pilgrims. Noon was its busiest hour with visitors eager to catch a glimpse of God. MVT security guards monitored the temple entrances but not to control crowds or preempt terrorist attacks. Rather, they were adamant enforcers of the *No shoes on holy ground* rule, a lesson most Christian children learn—and quickly forget—from the story of Moses and the burning bush.

For Indians, shoes are for flipping off at doorsteps and temple gates; rubber flip-flops suit visitors and residents well because they aren't too tempting for children to steal. But my soft feet don't care for flip-flops, going barefoot, or being dirty.

The noon walk to the temple was my first awkward attempt at strutting in my brown, plastic flip-flops. My feet felt vulnerable, unstable, and grimy with India's perpetual dust. But I was determined not to look like a brat, especially after my first effort at being open-minded failed over toilet paper.

I followed Fred with an insecure gait, entering the Vrindavan street on foot, which felt distinctly more clamorous than our initial ride into town in the security of a slow sedan. Rickshaws rushed by, overloaded with patrons and threatening to chop off my near-naked feet. Precious children spotted our white skin, pointed, and rushed toward us screaming, "Money!"

Fred hurried me along toward the temple and protected me from the children's and street vendors' pleas for my attention to buy something. *"Mataji!"* (mother or ma'am) they shouted, hoping I'd feel obliged to buy a trinket. I looked at the ground and avoided their calls and the children's grasps until we arrived at the temple's entrance.

SAFFRON CROSS

The slender men in blue security outfits outside of the temple pointed to my feet and grunted. I bent down to remove my clearance aisle flip-flops and came face-to-face with an old, emaciated, toothless woman dressed in white kneeling on the ground. She looked me directly in the eyes, moaned, and brought her leprotic stumps toward her mouth signifying her hunger. Her shredded white clothing indicated her place in Indian society as a widow, a designation forcing her to fend for herself and rely on the mercy of others. I wanted to collapse next to her in devastation.

Fred turned back and saw me bent at my waist, frozen as the widow continued to motion to her mouth. I was on the brink of a full-blown meltdown, and so he picked up my shoes and tenderly placed them on my feet as if I were a child while I stared helplessly back at her in silence.

"Let's go, my sweet."

Fred held me closely as we walked along the main road, his arms encircling me in a protective embrace as we made our way back to the room, where I hurled myself onto the pushed-together twin beds and lost all composure. He comforted me as I howled and remained in the fetal position until late afternoon, crying over the state of widows, my own ignorance and greed, and the overwhelming chaos that is India. I never forgot the widow because she had already been forgotten by so many.

When I finished shaking, I told Fred I was ready to go back out.

"You sure?"

"Yes."

This time I wore the old tennis shoes I snuck into our bag against Fred's advice and asked that we not go anywhere where I'd have to take them off. Fred obliged, and we made our way back to the main street and avoided holy spaces all afternoon. I looked straight ahead, stoically, amidst the calls of *Mataji* and begging. I decided that India's poverty was too crushing for me to focus on each thin child and pitiful woman dressed in white. I could be compassionate but would avoid being so overwhelmed that I could not function.

I assigned myself a mission, a goal that placed me back on the busy street but kept me focused. I needed a wool *chaddar* (blanket) to wrap around my head for modesty's sake and in preparation for Vrindavan's cool December mornings. Fred and I went to the nearest street vendor—steps away from the widow at the temple.

I knew that Indian businessmen increased all prices for Westerners. At the simple roadside stand, I told the vendor what I needed in Hindi and asked him how many rupees it would cost. He thought for a moment, calculating the extra profit he could gain from a Westerner's purchase. He offered me the *chaddar* at triple the price, and I bargained him down to close to a fair price for the simple dark blue and purple wool shawl.

I realized later that bargaining with an Indian businessman based on principles of Western discrimination was a ludicrous, consumerist thing to do. Who cared if he charged me three times as much? Any Westerner could afford India's inflated street prices. After two weeks in Vrindavan, my need for asserting my inner bargain-shopper would fade, giving way to the Eastern minimalistic and spiritual tendencies of this holy village.

In the days that followed the first messy afternoon, we found our Vrindavan routine—or rather it found us. We fell into the sacred rhythm of temple activities and simplicities.

I learned quickly that there was no hoarding in India. All meals were purchased (or cooked) one at a time, baths were taken one bucket at a time, and, in my crooked case, napkins were stolen one at a time. There was no endless supply of water and food; there were no stocked pantries and linen closets. There was only one of everything: one towel, one blanket, one bucket, one bar of soap, one cup, and one plate.

Fred and I relied on the safe vegetarian meals served by the ashram's restaurant, which offered food according to a set schedule, or *timings* as Indians call it. The restaurant offered no meals on fasting days, proving problematic for someone like me who is unaccustomed to religious fasts. But to eat from a street vendor in India is to risk eating food prepared in filthy conditions— and, according to local legend, deep-fried in recycled motor oil. What may suit the steel stomachs of Indians is a terror to the delicate American digestive system and can have detrimental effects beyond the visit.

Fred and I had packed one box of granola bars for expected times of food insecurity. When regular meals were offered at the restaurant, we bought a few extra *chapattis* (India's tortilla that sells for ten cents) that didn't need refrigeration and ate them for breakfast, snacks, or meals when ashram food was not available.

✝ ॐ ✝ ॐ ✝ ॐ ✝ ॐ ✝ ॐ ✝ ॐ ✝ ॐ ✝ ॐ ✝ ॐ ✝ ॐ ✝ ॐ ✝

The Krishna Balarama Mandir (temple) adjacent to MVT hosts thousands of visitors each year. Gaudiya Vaishnavas come here to worship Lord Krishna and visit Swami Prabhupada's *samadhi* (resting place).

The temple is a lavish structure drenched in bells and smells with black-and-white tiled marble floors and arches held up by large columns. The temple has no ceiling; the open-air space is covered only with thin black netting, allowing the sun's rising and setting to fill the holy space and keep time. Along the walls, colorful portraits depict scenes from God's pastimes (*lila*). There are three robust altars at the front, each with two life-size deities: Sri Chaitanya Mahaprabhu and Sri Nityananda Prabhu; Sri Krishna and Sri Balarama; and Sri Radha and Sri Krishna. God is never without a counterpart. Feminist theologians will be happy to know that God's female counterpart (Radha of Radha-Krishna) brings out the most intimate and sweet side of God.

Each afternoon, matronly women sit beneath these paintings among heaps of bright orange marigolds and string garlands for the deities. An adjacent temple kitchen prepares the deities' meals, the remnants of which are called *prasad*, or literally *grace*, and are consumed by the community. *Kirtan*, a traditional Indian devotional practice of chanting hymns or mantras, occurs 24-7 at the temple.

In the mornings, devout Gaudiya Vaishnava practitioners gather before dawn to pace along these walls and chant. Many Hindus vow to chant sixteen rounds per day on their *japa* (prayer) beads. Resembling rosaries, *japa* beads are usually made of the sacred plant tulsi. There are 108 beads per string, which makes for chanting a whopping 1,728 mantras of the Lord's Holy Names each day. The goal of this practice is to have a continuous, incessant absorption in the vocative repetition of God's name. Chanting sixteen rounds in the morning takes about two hours; this is why *japa* promptly begins at 4:30 a.m. The day begins with its rightful focus on God; prayers are said before the material distractions clutter your mind.

During our two-week stay, Fred woke up early to chant *japa* at the temple with the other devotees. He wore his *dhoti* (Indian man's pants) and *tilak* (yellow clay gathered from the banks of the sacred Yamuna River), drawn into a teardrop symbol indicating his Hindu sect. For American Christians, wearing *tilak* resembles the imposition of ashes and would be the equivalent of marking denominational affiliations on their foreheads.

Most *tilak* marks in Vrindavan indicate the Gaudiya Vaishnava tradition. This observable sign of faith is one of India's most charming rituals, demonstrating its status as a land of spirituality. Belief is not reserved for certain hours of the week; it is woven into the everyday fabric of community. *Tilak* on and wrapped tightly in his wool *chaddar,* Fred walked to the temple each morning to sit on what I deemed to be the world's coldest floor.

Most days, I got up too, though reluctantly. I began my days by praying for a hot cup of coffee to magically appear as a gift from Jesus—my due for enduring a honeymoon with no heat, no sex, and limited hot water. The coffee did not appear, so I begrudgingly pulled on my layers of leggings, pants, two pairs of socks, camisole, long sleeve shirt, and fleece jacket. I wrapped myself in my newly purchased *chaddar* and clutched my orange and green Indian flag journal, an early Christmas present from Fred, and shuffled in my flip-flops to the temple (with socks this time—a trick I learned that sustained me).

Even during India's coldest months of December and January, hardly anyone wears a coat. Poverty is one reason for this bizarre practice; being a colorful, joyful people is the other. In India, it's much more acceptable to wear mismatching layers of saris and *chaddars* that boast swirls of rainbow colors than a boring winter coat. This is India's paradox—vibrancy amidst heartache.

The first ten minutes at Krishna-Balarama Temple were always the worst. I never seemed to have bundled up enough to survive the distractingly cold floor. No caffeine and others' pacing and chanting the Lord's name at 4:30 a.m. irritated me. Grumbling, I propped myself up against the temple wall, opened my journal, and prayed for God to grant me a charitable heart.

I wrote page after page in the dark, huddled against the humming structure. I reflected on India and Hinduism and all the things I loved and loathed about my honeymoon. I wrote about how I felt myself changing and that the glimpses of India's beauty, poverty, and devotion reminded me of Christ. Jesus seemed so much more accessible in Vrindavan with no commercials or shopping centers blocking him out. He was here—in the poor widow's mangled limbs, the children's cries, and the early morning prayers of devotees. This interfaith honeymoon was going to deepen my Christian path in ways I hadn't imagined. While I wrote, my backside turned numb, the hushed chant of prayers no longer frustrated me, and the temple became slowly drenched in the soft light of dawn.

I usually got in at least one round of chanting the Lord's Holy Name—as I was supposed to be doing—but was far more successful at filling the pages with early morning musings. Before we left for India, Fred gave me the first pair of *tulasi japa* beads he used as a monk. I kept them in a white tattered bead bag hung around my neck. Fred's prayer beads were worn, indicative of years of devotion and practice. They were infused with spiritual energy, and years after our Indian honeymoon, a Christian friend and cancer survivor would hold them and say, "You can *feel* the Divine in these." When I prayed with them in Vrindavan, I could picture Fred's simple, disciplined monastic days in my mind's eye. I wore them each day we were in India; they manifested the reality of what a unique gift of immersion this interfaith honeymoon was.

During 4:30 a.m. *japa* time when I did harness the focus to pray, I chanted the *Maha Mantra,* the Lord's Holy Name, a common prayer used by the Gaudiya Vaishnavas. At other times, I struggled to remember Bible verses I learned as a child. When my memory failed me (as so often it did), I recited the Lord's Prayer, the Jesus Prayer, and Hail Mary.

Enthralled with Vrindavan's devotion, I fell into this daily *japa* routine, abiding by a schedule not of my own making in a land where I was the other. I was impressed that the Vrindavan residents' lives revolved around God's schedule—and not the other way around. No one complained. The devotees just *knew* that their moments belong to God. They accepted it as their *dharma* (duty), and this duty evolved into love. So many mornings on the cold temple floor I wished Protestants felt like this and prayed liked this. No Baptist I knew was praying 1,728 prayers per day. After a week's worth of early morning prayers, my ego got the best of me, and I felt a burst of self-righteousness for awakening early and merging two religious worlds under the open-air netting of a marble temple. But this superiority evaporated quickly when I realized a honeymoon's worth of piety did not make me like the devoted, day in, day out Hindu pilgrims who surrounded me.

After *japa*, Fred and I returned to our room to prepare for the MVT restaurant's hefty 8:30 a.m. breakfast. We planned the day's adventures over a plate of potato *parathas*, fresh yogurt, wheat oatmeal, juice, and ginger tea. Most days, we chose temples to visit, as Vrindavan is home to nearly five thousand of them, ranging from the roadside hut to the grand Krishna-Balarama Mandir.

Within the first few days of arriving, Fred purchased a full-color book on Vrindavan from the temple store. We used this book to map out where we wanted to go, and we prepared ourselves for the stress of each journey. Even going a few miles in India is a hassle; the roads and vehicles are not conducive to leisurely travel and afternoon strolls.

After breakfast, I packed our small bag for the day, having saved half of our *parathas* and *chapattis* for lunch. We left MVT's gates for the busy dirt road. By now, I had grown accustomed to the begging, nagging, and staring brought by the inhabitants of the main road. As was evident by the first afternoon's *chaddar* purchase, Fred discovered that I was good at asserting myself with Indian businessmen, so he assigned me the responsibility of securing our bicycle rickshaw rides to the Loi Bazaar, Vrindavan's marketplace. I took my communication cues from the matriarchs of the village. When Indian men came under the bossy fire of their mothers or female elders, they shaped up quickly. I tried to channel their maternal forcefulness. Most days, it worked.

I bargained for rickshaw rides several times per day depending on where we were and how tired we had become. Like New Delhi, walking Indian streets was exhausting. They were crowded—pedestrians fought rickshaws, cars, carts, and bulls for space to walk. Loi Bazaar market always buzzed with the energy of residents' daily shopping. The market too was where the Westerner got a glimpse of India's age-old battle of humans versus monkeys.

At MVT, guards in blue security suits walk the grounds carrying sticks and large slingshots to shoo away the aggressive monkeys. The ashram gardens are home to a sign that reads, *Beware. Monkeys may attack without warning.* In the market, this situation was intensified as there were no guards with big sticks to curb monkey misbehavior.

On our first trip to the Loi Bazaar, Fred and I saw hundreds of monkeys perched along store rooftops, poised to steal patrons' eyeglasses and hats to hold ransom for snacks. These furry thieves were scolded by angry shopkeepers, who promptly shooed away the rascals for fear they would eat all the shops' profits and drive away customers.

Because Hindus live strictly by faith rules of vegetarianism and not killing animals (*ahimsa*), they do not implement animal control to combat the overpopulation of monkeys. There is no segregation of humans and animals; creatures of all shapes and sizes are allowed to wander the streets. Pigs, wild street dogs, goats, cows, and bulls shuffle along the dusty paths, demanding the right-of-way from humans as they search for discarded food.

Considered to be the most sacred of animals in Hinduism, cows are the sweetest animals in the village. Cows are well-respected because of their gifts of milk, curd (cheese), yogurt, *ghee* (clarified butter), and fossil fuels. But cows who stop producing these goods—usually due to malnourishment—are abandoned on the market streets to fend for themselves, not unlike India's widows. This accounts for the majority of untied cows roaming about the village.

Fred and I crossed paths with the cows throughout our day's adventures, and I watched in amazement as these vagabond animals grumpily bucked past me to nuzzle against Fred. They adored him. These auspicious animals behaved as if they, in some mystical connection, knew of his monastic past and care for temple cows.

Each day, we roamed the village and visited ancient temples. Some were colorfully ostentatious and easy to find while others were hidden in urban nooks and required guides to pull you through stone mazes. Each temple held deities, or representations of God. Some deities were painted rocks and footprints in stone; others were statues less than one foot tall, while the more prominent temples' deities were life-size marble figures.

Mystic moods and hypnotizing incense bathed Vrindavan's temples. Spirituality invigorated the town; each altar made your heart warmer than the last. God's presence was obvious and strong—the Holy Spirit lived and breathed in each representation of the Divine. Vrindavan's religious sites affected me in the same way that silent, empty sanctuaries make me feel that

God is in the room. One cannot escape Vrindavan's holiness; it's more inviting than the billboards advertising luxury condos on the busy main street.

In India, no one asked if I were a Christian, and I didn't disclose. Instead, the village had unknowingly embraced our interfaith living as real and ripe, and I learned my second interfaith lesson: no one needed me to distinguish my faith from Fred's. There was only one, true, proper Divinity in Vrindavan, a force you were connected with no matter your spiritual path.

As Fred and I visited temples and markets, I continued to experience the heartbreak of India's poverty, which differs greatly from America's impoverished. It affected me at my core—one of the many important spiritual awakenings learned on the other side of the world. Most village residents were malnourished; they endured daily food and water insecurity and had no indoor plumbing or proper sewage system. They bathed in the streets at public water pumps. Children who did not attend school played with trash and feral puppies.

Families lived in shacks crafted from plastic bottles. Someone told me Vrindavan residents actually have to pay rent for their trash tents and the roadside land on which they rest. In the evenings and early mornings, the village air filled with wood smoke, an indication of the small fires that blazed outside these huts. These fires—no bigger than manholes—warmed those who squatted around them and served as the only source of light and heat until daybreak.

Other malnourished Vrindavan residents are dressed in saffron and white, an indication of their place in society as *sadhus* (holy men voluntarily committed to austerity) or widows, both of whom rely solely on the generosity of others. Almost everyone in India is thin, making the American spare tire an embarrassment of riches—and quite shocking upon returning home.

During our two weeks in India, I became more accustomed to simplicity; to one of everything; to dirt, bucket baths, electrical outages, food and water insecurity, and a schedule not of my own making. And I remembered Christ who said, "Foxes have holes, and birds of the air have nests; but the Son of Man has nowhere to lay his head" (Matt. 8:20).

Immersion in the birthplace of this ancient Eastern tradition shifted my Western, Protestant, materialistic perspective. India became a rejection of the tiny world I knew; I began to grasp the depth and breadth of the ways God had shown up for the rest of the world. The revelation of Hinduism as a daily framework of humble service to God was exactly the context Fred wanted me to see. It was now clear why he chose Hinduism, or why it chose him.

Our interfaith honeymoon, with its New Delhi chaos, Vrindavan sweetness, and absence of sex marked the beginning of a fledgling, Christian-Hindu marriage. Two weeks of study, practice, and placing God in the center of our lives brought Fred and me closer and cemented our commitment to each other and our shared path. It fueled us for the difficult road ahead of navigating household, sabbath, dietary, and theological differences. It set our course with a focus on the One who created us both and by whose grace we were brought together to navigate the challenges of an east-meets-west relationship.

In India, my initial and lingering assumptions and hesitations about interfaith relationships began to shatter. Immersion into a religious tradition different from my own did not convert me, mix me up, or derail me. Rather, it launched my Christian reformation—a recommitment to my baptism, my call, and my choices. It was easy to forfeit sex and daiquiris for such grace.

Fred and I returned to our one-bedroom apartment in North Carolina in solidarity and dedication to this atypical path. We brought Vrindavan's messy boundaries with us: the fusion of life and church that begins and ends with daily remembrances of the Divine.

Dried temple garlands rest in a glass jar on a dark wooden bookshelf that serves as our home altar. A silver *om* purchased in the Vrindavan marketplace dangles from my neck most days, gently tapping against the cross I wear on the same chain—two outward symbols of an inner mystery. They remind me of that holy space seven thousand miles away where Fred and I fused our interfaith marriage—and where God is inescapable.

Our journey began two years before the Indian adventure when visions of lonely future holidays spent as Bridget Jones propelled me to join a national dating site for matching soulmates. I hadn't bought stock in the outcome; it was difficult imagining that answering a complex personality survey of musthaves and can't-stands on a gray day would manifest a miraculous result. But it all began with the click of a box—and the Universe took note.

CHAPTER

eHARMONY

*Love is an endless mystery, because there is no reasonable cause
that could explain it.*

Rabindranath Tagore

While the rest of America digested fried turkey, I sat at a computer in the
apartment I shared with my mother and checked several hundred boxes
describing my temperament, habits, likes, and dislikes. I pored over endless squares indicating my desires in a partner: values, physical attributes,
habits, spirituality, religion—or lack thereof. I worked hard to spare myself
from psychopaths and smokers, and moved onto more sacred matters.

The eHarmony television commercials enticed me. The silver-haired
Dr. Neil Clark Warren boasted that, for the price of a pair of shoes, his
lengthy questionnaire would help me meet the love of my life. Happy,
attractive couples careened across the screen, and I yearned for relief from
the approaching holiday season, which was hell for a self-proclaimed spinster whose college and divinity school friends were already celebrating
fifth anniversaries and working on child number two.

Dr. Warren is a clever devil. His dating service sets itself apart from the competition with this dissertation-length survey that includes the added component of matching folks by faiths not limited to Christianity.

"What faith(s) would you accept in a partner?" the eHarmony algorithms inquired.

My dating history had been insularly Christian, save for the nonpracticing Muslim medical student I dated briefly while in college.

What would I accept? I wondered.

I ticked off *Christian* and *Jewish* without delay and narrowed the field. The Jewish bit was no surprise; I felt kinship with my Hebrew brothers and sisters, along with a lifelong infatuation with Adam Levine lookalikes. But the remaining traditions? I bit my lip. How did I feel about *Muslim, Buddhist, Hindu, Spiritual, but not religious, Agnostic,* and *Atheist*?

The last two were out; it would be difficult to bridge the gap between a Christian minister and someone who wasn't, at the very least, seeking God. The global traditions remained, and I looked out the window in search of an answer. The glass reflected a woman sitting in her pajamas at three o'clock in the afternoon with no Saturday night date. My pool of suitors was shrinking, and as far as I was concerned, I was one inch closer to turning forty-five and having twenty-nine cats. I needn't decrease my chances further by being picky about the ways in which a future beau approached God.

"All remaining world religions? Sure." I ticked them off one at a time, whispering to myself, "The possibility that I'd be matched with anyone who isn't a Christian is minute, right?"

"Right," God giggled.

Religion was the least of my worries anyway. Anxiety had already set in for the next, excruciating step of online dating: the personal profile and its photo. What can you say about yourself that is not awkward when you are an aging female Southern Baptist minister who still lives with her mother? The task of crafting an online dating profile produces the worst writer's block known to this generation. I awoke my orange tabby cat, Truffy, from his nap to talk it through.

"What do you think would make me attractive to an online dater?"

Truffy eyed the flowered pajamas I'd worn since the sixth grade and noted my thick glasses and uncombed hair. He was unimpressed.

"Let's make this quick as I have business that requires my attention," I thought I heard Truffy say. "Don't list Jesus as your best pal or mention that you sleep with a Bible under your pillow. You are not a domestic goddess nor do you exercise regularly. Rather than having a confident personality, you teeter on the edge of constant neediness. Should you be tempted to offer any falsehoods or pretenses, remember that you will be subsequently struck by lightning, in which case finding a soulmate will be moot anyway."

I worked on crafting a harmless, generic narrative about myself that was mostly true. I wrote about engaging with others in sincere ways and that I was looking for a man who noticed the details. I made a quick reference to a theological degree and nervously explained it away as not something you come across every day. I did my best to avoid writing, "I'm a single, Christian minister clinging to the ledge of my twenties and my eligibility. Nice to meet you."

The next, equally ulcer-inducing step was choosing a profile photo. Full body or head shot? Flattering photo from ten years ago when things were still firm and in their place? Or recent photo depicting gravity's evil ways and seven stressful years of desk-sitting for undergraduate and graduate degrees? I hadn't produced a good photograph since I was eighteen. The Baptist church directory picture taken that previous winter was the closest I was going to get to a well-lit, well-shot photo.

A local portrait studio that excels in arranging family awkwardness took our church directory photos. When I arrived for my appointment on a dateless Friday night, the photographer dragged his metal stool close and studied me carefully. I was thirty pounds overweight and wore a colorful blouse I hoped would conceal that fact. My hair was pulled back in a bun so tightly that it made my head look shrunken against my broad shoulders. The photographer sighed loudly, leaped atop his chair, and placed his lens four feet above my head in an attempt to create some semblance of a jawline. Bless him.

The photographer scowled at the digital preview and didn't hide his frustration. For the second try, he positioned my curled right hand under my chin in a classic graduating-high-school-senior pose. I had nothing left to do but show him and the entire world my only physical prized possession: thirty-two perfect teeth saved by orthodontia.

I uploaded this Mona Lisa to my eHarmony profile, made it public, and turned on the matching option. I prayed for compassion as I flung my virtual self out into the ether for the online dating robots to do their jobs and tell me with whom I would share coffee—or the rest of my life. Days later, I received six matches, and the impending holidays seemed a little brighter.

The first match to arrive in my eHarmony mailbox was a thoughtful looking man named Fred in a sepia-toned photo. He wore a dark shirt, relaxing on a couch with his left arm on the back edge, elbow bent and hand pressed to his head. He looked toward the right side of the room with a contemplative smile. His profile read like a novelist's carefully crafted character sketch of a well-meaning protagonist.

"I'm passionate about making a real difference in the world by understanding people in their social, economic, and spiritual contexts; connecting with people (and connecting them with others) through honest dialogue; and perpetually rediscovering the beauty of life in art, music, and the human condition."

I'd never seen a man articulate such an understanding of the world and humanity. Most men I knew, had they had any of these sorts of insights, would have stuffed them behind camouflage, hunting rifles, and tailgating. But the man on the screen said the most influential person in his life had been a monk who "helped me think critically and objectively about myself, the world, and the relationship between the two."

It got better. He "appreciated eccentric personalities" (fortunate for me), loved breakdancing, and loathed materialism. A renunciative dancer who tolerates quirky people? I continued scanning his profile for more essentials: "spiritual, but not religious;" "maybe" for wanting children; and nonsmoker. The "influential monk" piece confused me, but I waved off any concern. He was probably Catholic or had a mentor who was.

Per the eHarmony system, I knew he had also viewed my profile, but he hadn't reached out. My self-talk made me older and uglier by the hour, but I remembered *The Rules*, an ancient piece of dating literature I read in high school that placed men in the driver's seat of courting rituals. I bided my time with other boring eHarmony matches whose profiles all similarly listed Jesus and NASCAR as their main interests. I grew anxious waiting for the most thoughtful man I'd never met to contact me. Visions of another lonely New Year loomed, and I knew I'd soon be wrinkled and covered in cat hair.

When yet another worry line surfaced on my forehead, I decided that I'd rather die an aggressive, shameful twenty-first-century woman than a cat lady, and I sent Fred an innocuous eHarmony message asking about his work as an IT systems administrator. I'd save the monk inquiry for another day.

He responded within five hours, and I was equally shocked and thrilled. He gave the standard details of his North Carolina State University (NCSU) position and asked about my work in "higher education."

Feeling I had nothing to lose, I decided to come clean about my Master of Divinity degree and job at Duke Divinity School. I snuck my ordination in the last sentence like a suburban housewife telling her husband she'd spent the week's grocery money on a cashmere sweater. My clergywoman status didn't go unnoticed, and Fred confessed that he too was ordained and had been a priest and monk. But his explanation included a twist I hadn't expected: he was Hindu. The message closed with this disclaimer.

"I realize the fact that I was a Hindu monk might put you off, but I'd like to emphasize that I have taken from that experience a very holistic view of spirituality, a deep respect for all traditions, and an ability to see the common thread that runs through them."

"How do I feel about this?" I asked both myself and Truffy aloud.

I felt ambivalent; even my Duke Divinity School classmates couldn't have conveyed their spiritual journeys and ecumenical philosophy with the sensitivity Fred displayed on his profile and messages. But he didn't believe in Jesus? Still, it appeared that this was a man who'd spent years learning about himself, God, and the world. I had only encountered such spiritual depth previously when I read writings of the desert fathers.

I considered that perhaps it wouldn't be such a big deal. After all, I had checked the world religions boxes on the eHarmony matching system days ago when I was desperate not to limit my dating pool and hadn't imagined my openness would bear fruit. My exposure to Hinduism had been minuscule but moving. For my university's religion and philosophy requirement,

I took Eastern Traditions with a mellow Mennonite professor who taught barefoot. My intrigue—even with a non-Christian—was enough to carry the momentum.

We exchanged more messages, and I pictured Fred in a friar's woolen robe huddled in a stone cell, contemplatively meditating on the Divine and answering my questions about his spiritual journey. The theological and spiritual connection—albeit from vastly different perspectives—was electric. I wanted to know everything about the man in the sepia photo.

Fred lived in Raleigh, just thirty minutes from my Chapel Hill apartment. He asked for my telephone number to arrange a lunch date between our two cities, and I felt my destiny shift. We met in person just before Christmas at a small restaurant near Duke University. When I arrived, Fred was seated outside at a black wrought iron table reading *Indy Week*, our local progressive arts paper. He exuded attractive detachment with a light-blue collared shirt, navy-blue pants, and a dark hoodie. His chestnut hair and icy blue eyes were set off by an angular jaw line that sat atop the quintessentially skinny figure of a veteran vegetarian. I wore a trying-too-hard bright red cable knit sweater and equally loud lipstick.

Fred and I greeted each other with a handshake and moved bashfully inside the restaurant. Our waiter buffered first-date exchanges with third-party conversational kindnesses, and we ordered vegetable quesadillas, which we barely touched because of our incessant talking. He explained the discovery of consciousness that led to his collegiate Eastern philosophical studies and the path to the monastery. I asked about the intricacies of Hindu worship—which, stereotypically, most Christians viewed as Old Testament idolatry. He inquired about my journey to divinity school and current service to a church, and I offered the testimony of personal and professional baggage that every female Southern Baptist minister living into her pastoral identity can recite by heart.

I studied him as we talked, wondering at the small scar on his forehead and at the mystical force behind a man with such an intuitive nature. He confessed that he was just one-and-a-half years out of Hindu monastic service, a detail I tucked away to ponder later. We listened intently to each other's Christian and Hindu histories; he'd tell me later that he had never been able to discuss spiritual topics so freely with anyone outside the monastery.

I could have talked with him all day, but the date did eventually come to an end. He walked me across the street to my car in the soft December rain, gave me a strong hug, and wished me a Merry Christmas.

My half of the hug lingered too long, and I disappointed dating coaches everywhere by asking, "You're going to call me, right?" He smiled and said that he would.

We went our separate ways for the holidays, and I knew I'd be an old cat lady before he would call. I traveled to the beach with my mother to visit my aunts, who lovingly calmed my neuroses and encouraged me to pray. I paced the dark beach and begged God for a second date with the former Hindu monk.

Please God, I don't ask for much, I lied. *If you give me a second date with him, I promise I'll read my Bible.* That was a lie too, but God had a sense of humor, and the joke was on me. I'd soon be encouraged to crack open the text as I chased answers to Fred's complex theological questions.

When Fred called the day after I offered my beach promises and asked for dinner and movie the following week, I blew God a kiss and sat down to brush up on John's Gospel.

The candlelit restaurant adjacent to NCSU's campus offered a pleasant backdrop for second date theology on New Year's Day. The stakes felt higher, and I prayed through each bite of my meal. Our faith connection was as powerful as it had been in our initial meeting—with little time wasted on trivial topics.

Up to this point, I'd lived my entire faith journey with like-minded Christians, who, for the most part, espoused a similar theological construct. My faith matters had never been challenged from a contrasting paradigm, but Fred's Hinduism meant I was no longer fussing with fellow Christians over whose baptismal method was superior or whether connectional systems were more efficient than autonomous congregations. Instead, I was exploring the significance of sacraments and polity with a pilgrim whose faith perspective was intrinsically different from my own.

God became interesting again. Fred and I gobbled up theology the way Americans gorge on reality TV. I didn't delude myself into thinking that this newfound pull toward God hadn't been influenced by my physical and emotional attraction to Fred. It's possible that we could have discussed physics, and I'd still have been hooked. But never had such fascinating, intense theological conversations come my way, and never had I expected to have them with someone of another faith. My lifelong Christian practice had become rote, but Fred ignited a spark I hadn't felt since my baptism.

Fred asked difficult questions too—the kind that made me feel embarrassed at having a prestigious, expensive Master of Divinity degree and an inability to spew theological eloquence the way my classmates and faculty had. I grasped for church history tidbits on the development of the creeds. I kicked myself for daydreaming away Dr. Stanley Hauerwas's course in Christian ethics and felt a sudden nostalgia for barely surviving three years in Duke University's hallowed halls. I didn't know the answers to all of Fred's doctrinal inquiries, but I knew where to find them. I would become a thirsty student again, extricating knowledge among piles of scholarly volumes.

We finished our meals and walked to Fred's car. I was high on the Trinity—plotting which seminary books I'd drag off my shelves when Fred interrupted my thoughts.

"I just wanted you to know I have a date with another eHarmony match tomorrow night," he offered casually.

My knees buckled; I wanted to melt beneath his tires but had to recover quickly so as to not ruin any future chances I may or may not have with the former Hindu monk I'd become so fond of. I had forgotten that the well-oiled eHarmony machine was still in commission, churning out matches for Fred.

My internal life coach offered sage advice. *Stay in the moment, and we'll think (and cry) over this later. Best foot forward now. Make a good impression.*

"Cool," I responded aloud, hoping he couldn't detect my shaking voice and sad face in the dark. We got into his car and headed for the movie, and I distracted myself successfully for the remainder of the evening. The night ended with a kiss in the Whole Foods parking lot where he'd met me hours earlier.

On the drive home, I oscillated between feeling euphoria because of the best date I'd ever had and doom because of Fred courting another woman.

I am toast. Finished, I thought. I imagined the other woman was less of an insecure mess than I was. I cried for the next three days, picturing them together, mourning my unrequited love and spinster destiny. I had *finally* found an interesting, thoughtful man who loved God, and he was dating another woman. I obsessed and sobbed until Sunday night, when I checked my email and found a report of Fred's date in my inbox.

"She and I had no chemistry—not like you and I have."

Over the next few weeks, I continued my "let's-make-a-deal" game with God, offering bargains of prayer and scripture reading in exchange for time with Fred. Eventually, the prayers evolved and showed just a glimmer of maturity: I begged God to nurture our relationship through the gray days of winter, where spring tulips and Easter revelations awaited us on the other side. The former Hindu monk's influence was propelling me toward the Divine, without my even realizing it.

The next few months were a departure from my status quo life and spirituality. God called me to an adventure—romantically and theologically—with a man I hardly knew. Dating Fred marked the beginning of feverish desire for all things sacred. Initially, the spiritual shift was unconscious; I'd always felt I'd been close to God but from a perspective that made *me* the most important part of our relationship. When Fred talked about God on our dates, I felt like a presumptuous novice. I'd never made God the center of prayers, conversations, days, or service. I'd never brought the sense of humility and hunger that monastics pour before the Divine.

Fred's Eastern language of *What I can do for God* was a stretch for my individualistic theology of *What can God do for me?* I felt thirsty to serve Jesus again, a longing I hadn't encountered since the early years of my Christian walk. My budding relationship with a former Hindu monk brought with it an outcome I hadn't expected: a return to God.

CHAPTER

DATING AND INTERFAITH TENSIONS

Whether you want things, want nothing, or want salvation,
you must by all means worship the Supreme Lord.

Adapted from *Srimad Bhagavatam* 2.3.10

"Do you pray?" I asked innocently.

It was the most evangelical-flavored question I'd posed since we'd started dating.

Fred looked up from his cheese-encrusted legume.

"Excuse me," he replied as he left the table and headed straight for the men's restroom.

"Crap." I slumped back into my chair as he disappeared behind the wooden door. Deflation turned to panic.

Is he sick? Mad? Dana, what have you done? You've offended him. He hates you. Maybe prayer is not something Hindus practice. Now he's going to hide in the restroom the remainder of the evening until you finally get the hint and call a cab. This is a disaster.

I was scouting the room for an escape route when he returned, contemplative. I kept my mouth shut.

"I don't pray," he said. Full stop.

My heart sank. I resisted the urge to say, "What do you mean you *don't* pray? You were a monk!"

He read my mind and qualified the response.

"I don't pray in the way that *you* pray."

I gave him a puzzled look.

"Prayer is much different for Hindus."

I was still puzzled.

I wanted to know everything. How could prayer be so different? Had he ever prayed in the way that I assumed we all prayed—eyes closed, hands folded reverently, or prattling on to God about stress, dying loved ones, and dead-end jobs? But Fred's deep blue eyes told me I couldn't impose my urgency on the tension already between us. We weren't ready to address interfaith differences just yet.

I changed the subject and recentered us on a topic for which I knew we were on the same page: mutual love for complex worship liturgies. He smiled. I breathed.

✝ ॐ ✝ ॐ ✝ ॐ ✝ ॐ ✝ ॐ ✝ ॐ ✝ ॐ ✝ ॐ ✝ ॐ ✝ ॐ ✝

On my third date with Fred, we scooped red pepper lentils with Ethiopian *injera*, and I pressed for further assurances of our bond, hoping to forge a relationship strong enough to bridge our religious differences.

"It's just you and me right?" I inquired.

My feelings demanded that courting parameters be declared in person so that I could read his eyes for any hesitations.

"Just you and me," he replied, calm, confident, and unbothered by my leading question.

Fred's assurance would afford us safety and trust to revisit conflicts in the future. But it was weeks before I discovered why he fled to the restroom that night and what he meant when he said prayer was "different"

38

for Hindus. We had six dates under our belts before I had the courage to ask him, and I hadn't anticipated the explanation that demonstrated the intrinsic differences between the Christian and Hindu traditions.

I grew up with extemporaneous blessings before meals, invocations at the start of worship services, prayers for sick loved ones, merciful appeals for shut-ins, and petitions for offerings. No pastor I'd known read out of a prayer book; that was relegated to formal, mainline denominations. Instead, Southern Baptist clergymen were vibrant super heroes of supplication. Words from the Holy Spirit rolled from their tongues. Their prayers stirred my heart and brought tears to my eyes. I imagined everyone else grew up with the same elocutionary wizards and that they had been equally moved by their magic.

"Hindus don't have off-the-cuff prayers," he responded after I shared my description of prayer.

The bubble of my rural North Carolina existence burst when Fred went on to explain that extemporaneous prayers from Baptist pastors were actually the global exception, not the rule.

"Ideally, Hindus don't practice an aloud, spontaneous approach to God for things, people, meals, or healing," he said, and I detected just a hint of superiority. "The Hindu prayer routine is made up of chanting and is focused entirely on worship, devotion, and glorification of God. Prayer is centered on maintaining attention and devotion during these activities. Hindu prayers are based on scripture; there are no extra words that rely on human egos."

Fred's words stung, as if stream-of-consciousness wails for sick cats, job interviews, and second dates were foolish. The word *ego* echoed in my mind. I had always been the center of my prayer life with God; I usually prayed *Help me* sprinkled with the occasional *Thank you*.

"Dana, are you listening to me?"

"Sorry," I replied, snapping back to the present. "Keep going."

I had to concentrate, otherwise Fred would never get to exactly what made Hindu prayer so different from Christian intercessions.

"Hindu chanting is an appeal to God for help in serving and remembering him."

"So, no impromptu prayers for shoe sales or parking places?" I giggled nervously.

Fred sighed. I'd missed the point—I wouldn't get it until two years from this moment, when I was certain the faithful early morning chanting of Indian Hindus would launch the Krishna Balarama temple into the sky, propelled by the vibrant humming of the Lord's name.

"Hindus repeat God's Holy Name during their chanting on *japa* beads, like these." He pressed a long strand of wooden beads, worn and smooth as butter, into my palm. "They help keep you centered on adoration of God. It's like a Catholic rosary, but there are 108 beads instead of 59."

Fred's revelation of Hindu prayer fostered awkwardness deep inside me. Future blessings before meals and bedtime prayers for loved ones and better days would make me feel self-indulgent. But Fred insisted I continue with the Christian prayer tradition I had known my entire life. He made only one request: that I try chanting.

"You can chant anything you'd like—the Lord's Prayer, the Jesus Prayer, Hail Mary—and you can use my *japa* beads. Just please try it."

I couldn't imagine repetitive prayer would hold the same power for me as the thousands of unscripted conversations I'd had with God since the first time someone in my Protestant faith told me I could talk with God anywhere, anytime, and about anything. I'd built an entire faith practice on this foundation—me, with my rambling prayers, and God, listening patiently.

Our conversation left me wondering how Fred gotten to this point with prayer in the first place? How had he discovered this alternative framework for approaching the Divine that seemed stiff yet selfless? I needed answers, but this was only the beginning of theological differences yet to be addressed.

† ॐ † ॐ † ॐ † ॐ † ॐ † ॐ † ॐ † ॐ † ॐ † ॐ † ॐ †

"Do you accept Jesus as your personal Savior?" the pastor of a Baptist church asked.

"Yes," replied a sheepish twelve-year-old Fred, flushed with embarrassment and standing in full view of the congregation.

"Please repeat it, son."

"Oh, um, what was it again?" Fred stumbled.

Fred visited a Baptist church only a handful of times with his best friend from middle school. At Matt's urging, Fred reluctantly walked down to the front of the sanctuary during the last hymn, evangelical Christianity's first step to membership in the kingdom. Afterward, he met with the pastor.

"G-R-A-C-E. Grace is God's riches against Christ's expenses," the silver-haired pastor explained proudly.

An acronym of a financial metaphor for God's grace made Fred bristle.

In the space that could have held encouragement, direction, study, and guidance for spiritual practices, Fred instead received an accountant's explanation of salvation and a pat on the back. He felt empty. He was never baptized nor taught what it meant to live a Christian life.

But Fred continued on the Christian path laid before him and the rest of American youth growing up in the Bible Belt, wrestling alone with conflicts for which no one offered explanations. His earliest struggles with Christianity were twofold: a suffocating communal practice and what felt like an apathy toward actually putting biblical teachings into daily practice. Community worship choked him—it was seemingly a social gathering that catered toward extroverts who made introverts stand down front for professions of faith. He longed for contemplative practice but didn't know where to find it. Outside of worship, he couldn't reconcile why no one had allowed God to infiltrate his or her routines. Scripture reading and prayers were relegated to Sundays and hardly spoken of during the rest of the week.

Fred's teenaged perception of the obvious discrepancies between Christ's teachings and Christians' behavior made him hot with irritation. Mean-spirited believers who claimed to have been changed by the blood of the Lamb kept hardened hearts. Youth ministers preached a scary Jesus whose impending Judgment Day made pubescent girls sob. When God wasn't scary, God was portrayed as a vending machine, and Fred never met anyone whom he thought had truly tried to embody the love of Christ.

Spotty church attendance with Matt, an awkward altar call, and fear-inducing sermons marked the beginning and end of Fred's Christian practice. The church aggravated his faith and introversion; he'd felt nothing but distress during Christian encounters, something he intuitively knew couldn't accurately reflect the true nature of God. His middle school Protestant practice was over almost as soon as it had begun.

But Fred hadn't given up on finding out who God was and who he was in relation to God. He yearned for time and space to contemplate God's true nature in silence and without humanity's hang-ups. Fred was driven by the longing of a deeply personal faith experience rather than the communal, angst-ridden gatherings he had known. His unfolding spiritual path became characterized by discerning the tension of the internal and external worlds.

The conflict Fred felt between his teenaged material body and the supernatural culminated on a memorable Thanksgiving car ride to his grandmother's house when he was fourteen.

Why do I see through these eyes? Fred wondered as he looked through the window while the rhythm of the highway's dotted lines became a pulse of light and dark. *Why am I in this body?*

The cool car window pressed against his cheek, a sharp contrast to the warm seat beneath him. He'd lived his short life in philosophical dissimilitude—wrestling with the odd juxtaposition of spirit and matter. Now, the fall colors blurred along the interstate, creating a brilliant backdrop that fueled his realization of being a soul imprisoned in a body and looking out onto the world. He had discovered his consciousness. He was not his body; he felt immediate relief.

† ॐ † ॐ † ॐ † ॐ † ॐ † ॐ † ॐ † ॐ † ॐ † ॐ † ॐ † ॐ †

Each of our dates was propelled by the theological discussion of the last, and Fred slowly revealed the early details of his rejection of Christianity and discovery of Hinduism. He offered one Polaroid at a time, developed slowly and only in ideal conditions. He studied my reaction with each snapshot, sure I'd balk at one exposure, and we wouldn't be able to move to the next.

Fred's finding and leaving the Christian church, his middle school altar call, and his teenage discovery of consciousness in a car ride were the first memories he revealed. More sensitive matters—such as his decision to become a Hindu monk and priest, as well as his departure from the priesthood—surfaced later. His faith history was more tender and private than mine, which had been characterized by loving, supportive churches, family, and friends. As I patiently awaited a new scene in Fred's religious storyboard, I wore my own spiritual journey on my sleeve, offering happy memories of my early churches, followed by my subsequent internal struggles with the growing discrepancies of a progressive faith.

Once Fred disclosed his public profession of faith and the pastor's formula for grace, I offered a poor, insensitive response: my annoyance that he hadn't received proper follow-up, spiritual direction, and a baptism.

"Why didn't he baptize you?" I asked.

"I dunno."

"Would it have changed things?" I wondered aloud. "Would you have stuck with Jesus, if you'd had some encouragement and guidance? Would a baptism have made a difference?"

"No," he replied firmly. Christianity was not his spiritual path.

But the evangelical roots of my middle and high school formation at a Southern Baptist congregation sprouted from the conservative depths I thought I'd abandoned long ago. I felt anxious that Fred had not been baptized. I must have believed, without admitting it, that Jesus really was the only way. Though my liberal lips boasted the contrary, I deduced that a Christian salvation, complete with baptism, was the only method by which we could all go home.

† ॐ † ॐ † ॐ † ॐ † ॐ † ॐ † ॐ † ॐ † ॐ † ॐ † ॐ † ॐ †

The waters were cool beneath the white choir robes we wore. The drenched robes reminded me of the heaviness of life that even I had discovered by age eleven. I felt the weight of my parents' failed marriage, of being a lonely child whose only sibling was already a grown adult, and of my family's financial struggles. I felt relieved to drown all of it.

The other fifth graders, some middle schoolers, and I waited patiently in line on the concrete steps of the baptismal pool on Pentecost Sunday. The baptistry was a miniature swimming pool whose square, brick frame was wedged between the sanctuary and narthex. Above the water, a tall glass wall etched with a dove stretched the length of the fixture, and a hinged door allowed the minister and baptismal candidates through to face the seated congregants.

I had been waiting to partake in this sacrament since reading about the auspicious moment John baptized Jesus in the *Good News Bible* I received as a second grader. When it was my turn, I walked down the smooth steps and slid into the cold water, wading over to the female minister's arms. She held my back and asked me to profess my faith. Then she guided me under the water like an eloquent ballroom dance dip, all in the name of the Trinity.

I arose a new creation, with water dripping from my hair, face, and shoulders. The sanctuary was full of smiling congregants, including my mother, who was as happy to see me as she had been at my birth.

A deacon helped me emerge from the pool, dry off, and prepare to shake hands with the adults in the narthex after worship. I was a tiny eleven-year-old in a floral dress, with thick glasses and chin-length hair, but I felt sophisticated, like I was a part of something.

It had taken five long years to reach this sense of belonging. I had been an angry six-year-old when we moved from our Indiana chaos to Chapel Hill—a child who didn't understand why her father rejected her and why life was so unstable. The encouragement of the church's saints had helped me slough off my angry shell, and I found my place in the arms of the parish.

My baptism by a female preacher on Pentecost Sunday in one of the most progressive Baptist churches south of the Mason-Dixon was a spiritual lightning rod. Baptists tend not to be superstitious folk, but emerging from the waters in the arms of Rev. Wade on the most Spirit-filled Sunday of the liturgical year made God real and close, a watchful parent longing to see how her child's life will unfold.

The Olin T. Binkley Memorial Baptist Church had notoriety as a gathering of highly educated, community-minded advocates who were the hands and feet of Jesus' gospel. Binkley's reputation preceded it. When my mother and I told friends about our new church membership, they all offered the same knowing look. This was their acknowledgment of our association with the liberal, social-justice advocating, peacekeeping, inclusive language implementing believers who, to outsiders, looked more like Unitarians than Baptists. Even the building reflected the congregants' progressiveness; the light, airy sanctuary contained no stained-glass windows or choir lofts. It was lined with rose-cushioned chairs instead of pews. A large banner with the embroidered words *All Are Welcome* hung from the wall near the entrance to the building.

There wasn't a single copy of the King James Bible to be found on Binkley's grounds; instead, the standard translation of choice was *The Good News Bible*, distributed by the American Bible Society and birthed by principal translator and Binkley member Dr. Robert Bratcher. *The Good News Bible* was the beginning reader's gateway to the word of God, with simple sentences translated from original texts and black-and-white sketches that depicted important biblical scenes.

Dr. Bratcher was one among handfuls of scholars as well as social justice and civil rights activists who worked tirelessly for the disenfranchised and marginalized in the community. Reformers, historians, and ministers lined the chairs, upholding its charter members' mission of fostering a welcoming, diverse parish.

I couldn't intellectually grasp who these super-adults were, but I could feel their spirits in the aisles. They took Jesus seriously, modeling what the gospel really looked like. My progressive theological formation began among these saints.

Sitting next to these community champions were the everyday folks who benefited from their hard work: same-sex couples with young children, international refugees, and people of all colors and walks of life.

Before my parents' divorce and my revolutionary exposure to Binkley, my mother and I casually attended a Community Bible Church in Indiana where my paternal grandparents had been charter members. Since the day my parents saw my six-pound body in the delivery room, I had been groomed to follow a simple, unwavering Christian path. I never questioned the tradition of my birth nor the worshiping communities that nurtured me through my childhood and adolescence.

After the divorce, my mother knew a consistent church community would aid the transition to our new beginning. She grew up in a Southern Baptist congregation where Bible drills and missions were the heart of a traditional community. When we landed in Chapel Hill, she enrolled me in Binkley's children's program, a choice that diverged from her own rearing and the mid-Western congregations we had known. But Binkley reflected my mother's true being, which she hoped I would embrace as well: diverse, eclectic, and spiritually progressive.

Binkley's activities, children's choir, Sunday school, and worship calmed the chaos of our lives. I settled into the routine of being the daughter of a mother who worked weekend nights as a nurse at Duke University Medical Center. Sunday mornings, she'd drop me off before she slept off her twelve-hour night shift, or, when I was older, I'd cross the street from our rented condo and walk through the mall parking lot to Binkley's sanctuary. I found solace in a community of believers comprised mostly of recovering Southern Baptists from hostile upbringings I did not understand. I sensed that Binkley was a safe haven for folks who didn't belong anywhere else, which made me feel like I fit in perfectly.

But comfort was uprooted quickly as Chapel Hill's high cost of living, our financial struggles, and the diagnosis of my grandmother's Alzheimer's disease forced us to move to my mother's hometown and back to First Baptist Church, the Southern Baptist congregation of her childhood. Weeks following my Pentecost baptism, we packed a moving truck for a rural tobacco town where there were no Binkleys, no female ministers, and no *Good News Bibles*. Only my mother's childhood memories of a church that centered her simple, post-World War II existence remained, and I would be exposed to a new kind of faith and formation narrower than Binkley's outstretched arms. But Binkley's hold on me—its diversity, openness to different ideas about God, Christ, and the Bible—would have a lasting impression. A seed of openness had been planted—one whose veracity would bear important fruit.

✝ ॐ ✝ ॐ ✝ ॐ ✝ ॐ ✝ ॐ ✝ ॐ ✝ ॐ ✝ ॐ ✝ ॐ ✝ ॐ ✝ ॐ ✝

I wanted Fred to have the same Pentecost baptism moment I'd experienced in the unwavering love of Binkley Baptist Church. I was angry with the Baptist pastor of Fred's youth and his lack of guidance or insistence on Fred's baptism. I determined Fred's baptism was in order, and I was keen to do the duty myself.

The conservative facets of my Christian formation had gripped me tighter than I thought, and I hadn't yet grasped Hinduism's validity as a bona fide spiritual path toward God. I had succumbed to the Protestant anxieties and salvation formula of my teens: altar call + public declaration of faith + baptism into a community = saved. Fred hadn't completed the equation, and, should we stay together, we may not both make it to heaven. Fred was a sinner just like me, and I wanted to confirm his one-way ticket home to Jesus.

Growing up in a denomination that doesn't have a formal, high-church focus on sacraments meant that baptisms and Holy Communions were simple and symbolic. My Duke Divinity School Episcopalian, Catholic, and even Methodist friends would have croaked had they known my casual plans for adding Fred to the eternal roster.

Fred had actualized the first two steps in the process—his altar call and public declaration of faith—albeit reluctantly. I conjured all sorts of ways to complete the final step. I rationalized that it didn't have to be within a church community, and it didn't have to be perfect. After all, I was guilty of performing less-than-orthodox sacraments after divinity school when I served as a hospital chaplain.

I'd been paged many on-call nights to neonatal intensive care rooms at 2:00 a.m. When I arrived, concerned nurses shoved unused emesis basins and sterile water into my hands while anxious parents pleaded with me to baptize their tiny babies in the name of the triune God.

I didn't know these families, nor did I question how deep and pious their religious convictions were or whether they really were committed to raising this child, should it survive, in the church. But what I learned in those sacred moments is that the Holy Spirit always intercedes, and it is my job to get out of the way.

But Fred was a devout Hindu; he wasn't a dying baby. He'd been pressured into a middle school altar call, and he hadn't asked for a baptism. Still, in the few months I'd known him, I felt compelled to make his salvation complete, at least by my own standards. My timid dating disposition disappeared, and I took on the role of evangelical pastor. Not surprisingly, my offer was met with obstinacy.

"Why can't I baptize you?" I asked.

"Because I'm not a Christian!"

"But you are!" I protested.

"No, . . . I'm not."

"But you've *nearly* been saved," I pleaded. "You just need to complete the last step!"

Fred's eyes flashed with anger as I let "You've *nearly* been saved," fall from my tongue, and he knew instantly that I didn't view Hinduism as an equal religious path.

I'm not sure whose theology I was applying here, but my seminary professors wouldn't likely have approved of me pushing baptism on an unwilling candidate. This holy sacrament needed to be performed with the eager, with one who is ready to profess his or her faith in Jesus Christ, preferably with some discipleship classes and the witness of a community. My reluctant Hindu boyfriend did not fit the bill.

Still, I was adamant. I hadn't yet accepted Hinduism as a legitimate way to God. I was one of *those* Christians, the kind who couldn't see beyond her own nose to embrace a tradition that is, in fact, older than Christianity and steeped in sacred scripture, ritual, and authenticity.

I was forcing God (and Fred) into my cozy little Baptist box, and I continued to scheme before I finally let it go. I pondered baptizing Fred in his sleep or tossing water on his face at dinner and crossing him in the name of the triune God.

This was my first failed attempt at interfaith understanding.

Fred told me later that he'd had the Hindu equivalent of a baptism: first and second initiation, including receiving the *vaishnava deeksha mantra* when he was a monk. I wasn't sure what that meant until years later when I witnessed other Hindu devotees' initiations, and the Divine massaged their meanings into my heart. These rituals were as significant as any I'd ever known in the Christian church.

I moved on reluctantly and was eventually quieted with the notion that Fred didn't need to have the same salvific moment I'd had many years ago in the waters of Binkley's baptistry. Nor did Fred need the intense, biblical and theological formation I'd received in the First Baptist Church community.

My acceptance was a turning point in our months-old interfaith courtship; I understood Fred's Hinduism as a genuine path, as sacred and holy as any branch of Christianity. I relinquished what was quite possibly the last stitch of any conservative Baptist lingering. I opened myself to Fred's Gaudiya Vaishnavism, and I experienced a powerful shift: the more I exposed myself to beliefs outside of my own, the more my Christianity strengthened. In turn, Fred considered the benefits of stream-of-consciousness-prayer, particularly as he related it to dependence upon the Divine for his most basic needs.

†ॐ†ॐ†ॐ†ॐ†ॐ†ॐ†ॐ†ॐ†ॐ†ॐ†ॐ†ॐ†

Fred and I had overcome our different beliefs on prayer and baptism, but I couldn't shake the fear that Fred would return to his Hindu priestly vows. We had been dating only four months when I was admitted to our local hospital for emergency gallbladder surgery. The intensity of a five-day inpatient stay and Fred's bedside devotion told me our relationship was serious. But the escalation of our dating into a realm of long-term commitment scared me. I permitted myself to imagine the possibility of losing Fred back to the monastic life. Fred had never given me an indication of such; it was a symptom of my own worrying mind. Our relationship was happy, connected, and thriving when my self-sabotage surfaced. I just knew one day I'd receive an email outlining his urgent desire to return to life with his *guru* after rediscovering the annoyances of secular life. No such e-mail arrived, and Fred seemed as pleased with our growing seriousness as I was.

When Fred and I approached the six-month mark of our relationship, he asked me to attend my very first Hindu worship service that happened to coincide with a visit from his *guru*, Swami B. V. Tripurari. The event was held in the home of Alice and Mike, devout Gaudiya Vaishnavas. Home worship is a common practice in Hinduism; most devotees have altars of varying degrees, some with deities that require round-the-clock care and others with simple portraits of beloved *gurus* in saffron.

Fred had only seen his *guru* two or three times since leaving Audarya monastery. I sensed his nervousness about being in Swami's presence again; his agitation told me how much I still had to learn about Fred's priesthood and transition back to secular life.

That night, the two of us cooked up a story to ensure that Alice, Mike, and the other devotees knew we had only platonic energy, a device we enacted to avoid suspicions of the former monk having a new girlfriend.

In hindsight, our story was unnecessary. When the truth was later revealed, Fred's Hindu friends and monastic colleagues were excited (and curious) about him dating a Baptist minister. But before he could reach that point of comfort, Fred carried the monastic baggage that typically weighs down the public love lives of renunciates reentering the world.

I probably should have been offended by the tale that placed distance between Fred and me, but it offered me a spectator's buffer from which to witness my first deity worship. Our awkward posing also gave me a chance to observe the community's interaction with Fred. He had been away for a while, and it was important for him to reestablish himself in the group without further complications of a Protestant girlfriend. They cooed over his return, and it was evident how much they loved him.

We gathered in Alice and Mike's temple room, a garage finished with carpet and the coziness of a den. Their altar held two eight-inch tall deities, Gaura and Nitai, and photos of beloved *gurus*. The deities were immaculately dressed with jeweled outfits and colorful garlands. Spotlights illuminated their skin; their lotus-round eyes invited worshipers to focus on the Divine, like Orthodox icons offering windows to God.

I felt odd singing to what most Baptists deemed statues and, at the most fundamentalist level, idols. But I couldn't help but feel the Divine in their presence, the way I'd felt with the baptismal water at my chest or holding an oyster cracker and grape juice at the Lord's Supper. Christ was infused in these material symbols, and I recognized the shape of holiness.

We sang and prayed, and I asked God to wash the sound through me, bathing me in strength and patience for this budding interfaith partnership. I prayed too for the continued openness to fully accept Hinduism as a rightful path to God.

After worship, Swami taught a class that I could barely follow. It was steeped in robust philosophy and scripture; each sentence could have been its own sermon. I knew Fred was a devout, serious student, but I discerned from all the head-nodding and intricate questions that all of Swami's students embodied this level of commitment to the path, as that was the teacher's standard.

Two hours in, I squirmed inappropriately, having sat on the floor with crossed legs and numb feet. No one else wiggled; they were as disciplined in their bodies as they were in their intellect. I immediately felt guilty at my own lack of discipline. I hadn't studied the Bible the way they pored over the *Bhagavad Gita* and other Vedic texts, and I was terrified someone would ask me a question about Christian theology or the Gospels. I realized I was a Baptist among Hindus who probably knew more about my religion's precepts than I did.

At the conclusion of Swami's sermon, a sea of bodies parted and pressed their chests to the floor, offering obeisance as the saffron-cloaked priest passed. Swami paused only at Fred, just long enough to pat him gently on the head, like a father welcoming a beloved son home.

I had been formed well in my Christian tradition, taught the Bible and the tenets of my faith. But my theological muscles had gone soft as I had moved through subsequent phases of life, church, and divinity school without seemingly retaining much. I was a blank slate, feeling inadequate in comparison to Eastern practitioners steeped in their faiths, while I didn't know one-tenth of the doctrine of my own spiritual path. I'd left scripture and dogma behind when it became too complicated, too oppressive, too patriarchal; I hadn't yet returned. But the ghosts of my spiritual grooming emerged in this moment of Hindu connection, and I recounted the fingerprints of communities past filled with mentors and moments that molded me into who I would become.

CHAPTER

FORMATION

Teach children how they should live, and they will remember it all their life.

Proverbs 22:6, GNT

First Baptist Church was the 150-year-old architectural anchor of the streets of my mother's hometown. What began as a small chapel in 1844 flourished into a twenty-first-century ministry complex with a new sanctuary, fellowship hall, offices, educational wing, and youth area. Here my maternal grandmother and family matriarch steeped her five children in solid Christian ethics. Our family haunted the First Baptist membership ledgers for over seven decades. We were as devoted to the community's literal and figurative bricks as its charter members had been when the foundation was set.

I was eleven when I returned with my mother to her maiden name and her hometown. The moving boxes were still stacked in the corners of our apartment when I worshiped at First Baptist for the first time.

First Baptist Church looked nothing like Binkley. The broad, square sanctuary was lined with dark wood and golden-cushioned pews that matched the carpet below. Stained-glass windows depicting biblical stories stoically lined the walls. The pipe organ and pulpit were center stage. A long table just below the pulpit served as the traditional altar for a quarterly Communion of grape juice and oyster crackers and, more importantly for antisacramental Baptists, a weekly receiving area during the invitational hymn. The choir loft was elevated behind the organist's perch, raised and proud. The baptistry was a second-story bathtub that floated celestially, hidden behind a waist-high brick wall. It was accessible only by secret stairs behind shimmering organ pipes. In the next years, I would spend long afternoons alone wandering this complex, brushing my hands against its intricacies. In those silent hours, I could feel the Divine in the nooks and crannies.

Structural discrepancies aside, First Baptist had one glaring distinction from Binkley Baptist Church: everyone who warmed the pews looked the same, and the congregants were likely (at least publically) of the same political, theological, social, and sexual orientation. Binkley's rainbow of worshipers held religious convictions as individual as their skin tones. The two churches were separated only by two counties, but a cultural continent divided them.

Preaching the Bible was the bedrock of the First Baptist Church community. I'd never experienced a community whose sacred text was as primary and powerful. *The Good News Bible* was authoritative but understated; it didn't force itself on readers. Instead, it waited for inspired second graders to open its cover. It was never used as an instrument of coercion but as an invitation to a more thoughtful spirituality centered on the Old and New Testaments. I discovered that Binkley had been the exception to this rule: most Baptist churches thrust scripture upon children and teens with fear-based preaching and aggressive evangelism. First Baptist Church, thanks to its pastoral leadership, fell somewhere in the middle—not as leisurely as Binkley in its pursuits to get children to read the Bible, but not as strict as many of my Christian school friends had it.

The Trent family was interwoven in the First Baptist structural, contextual, and communal threads. Aunts, uncles, and near and distant cousins lined the third and last pews of the sanctuary's center left section, and I'd never been surrounded so intensely by kin. Our Indiana life had been too tumultuous for me to appreciate my paternal family, and in Chapel Hill, my brother, eighteen years my senior, was a busy Duke University medical student who graduated two years after my mother divorced my father.

The deep roots of the Trent family immediately had me grasping for connections, the same kinds of connections I reluctantly let go of at Binkley. As the weeks passed, I was instantly fearful my newfound feelings of belonging among Trents would be ripped away from me. I wasn't quite twelve, but I had already learned that change was the only constant in life.

But First Baptist Church and the Trent family became the congenial arms that Binkley had been. The week after I worshiped there for the first time, the unofficial First Baptist Church welcome committee named Delores Kinston knocked on our apartment door sporting gold flats and a smooth Southern drawl. She whisked me off to "Mac-Donald's" for a cheeseburger lunch, Christian hospitality, and descriptions of all the sixth grade programs. Delores had already informed the Sunday school teacher I'd never met that I'd be arriving soon. She said that she had also held a spot for me in her choir and handbell group and would help ease my eventual transition to seventh-grade youth group. Christlike kindness was embroidered on Delores's shiny exterior, and it made starting over feel less scary.

Our apartment was a short walk from the sanctuary doors, a clever move for a mother who wanted her daughter at church any time the lights were on. The First Baptist Church congregation had a tradition of ensuring its post-baptism fledglings were well-formed and well cared for but through an intrinsically different lens than Binkley's progressive theological tendencies. I joined the constant buzz of Wednesday and Sunday activities for the congregation's youngest members—a real boon to an aging tobacco town with nothing else going on and too much opportunity for teens to get into trouble.

I went willingly and earnestly to church because parents and leaders were friendly and programs were overflowing with grounded Christian kids. I met my lifelong best friend Kate standing by Delores Kinston's piano in sixth-grade choir practice, a debt for which I feel I owe First Baptist a limb. Kate and I, as well as the other middle school girls, grew fond of most church activities because the spiritual cake came with icing: the attention of the older youth-group boys.

My mother took a weekday job as a county health department nurse, which meant our lives had some semblance of a normal schedule. In lieu of expensive dance lessons, tennis, or the other activities kids who lived in two-income households partook of, I participated in church activities: choir, handbells, youth group, mission groups, Bible studies, and church-wide committees. The nearly two-centuries old congregation became my spiritual and social mainstay.

By seventh grade, saintly shepherds like Delores Kinston, the First Baptist ministry staff, lay leaders, and countless parents brought me into the fold and formed me beyond my comprehension. Caring adults encircled me, nourishing an awkward preteen whose only place of belonging was a house of worship. Their vested interest puzzled me; they bent over backward to keep and guide me on the path of Christian discipleship. Later, I discovered that their soft smiles and knowing nods were outward signs of the mystical, internal spiritual gifts they saw emerging in me.

But First Baptist's formation came at a cost: it was distinctly less broad-minded than Binkley. Through no fault of its own, the church was placed within a cultural context that housed traditional Southern Baptist roots. I absorbed the conservative aspects of the faith, my teen brain unable and unwilling to differentiate my current church experience from the wide, open world.

† ॐ † ॐ † ॐ † ॐ † ॐ † ॐ † ॐ † ॐ † ॐ † ॐ † ॐ † ॐ †

Fred discovered his own soul on a Thanksgiving road trip to his grandmother's house. By then he'd left the Christian church to seek God in other spaces, and his fourteen-year-old revelation of consciousness taught him that his essence was so much more than his body and the materialism that surrounded him. That vivid realization shaped his teen years, and what began as a general dissatisfaction with the world was now a full-on resentment of all things superficial.

The hometown Christianity Fred stumbled upon was no longer an option. Its peripheral and social focus that showed no desire for a deep,

integrated relationship with Christ frustrated him. But his teenage religious dissatisfaction evolved into spiritual assertiveness. He pioneered his
own quest for God, turning to the crumbling pages of old philosophy texts
in hopes of making meaningful spiritual connections. He didn't know how
the path would unfold; he only knew he hadn't liked where he had been.

After high school, Fred entered the University of North Carolina at
Greensboro (UNCG) and studied Information Systems. He stayed on a
steady academic path, fueling his problem-solving mind with complex
technology courses while deepening his philosophical search.

To supplement his college living, Fred took a part-time second shift
job at the Department of Transportation (DOT) watching highway cameras. Hours of quiet traffic time offered silence to devote to studies and,
during summer breaks, months to delve into philosophy. The Christmas
before he began the DOT job, he discovered Ralph Waldo Emerson's 1841
essay titled "The Oversoul," a Western text with Eastern influences. Fred
fixed himself on Emerson's exploration of the relationship between the
soul and ego, the soul and other souls, and the soul's relationship with
God. It mirrored what he had already ascertained along the highway: he
was not his body—and that felt like such a relief to him.

From there, Fred studied Theravada Buddhism and the *Yoga-sutras* of
Patanjali. In these practices he found more of what he was looking for:
a comprehensive description of the spiritual side of life and a concrete
means to live it. He was greatly affected by the directives of Eastern practices, including vegetarianism, which he found to be a common spiritual
practice among nearly all the Eastern texts he read. He gave up meat, fish,
eggs, and gelatin as a first step to a newfound focus on his soul. From
there, he quit smoking and longed to meet serious practitioners.

Divine providence intervened. Shortly after Fred's dietary conversion,
he heard a UNCG campus radio advertisement about local Hindus offering a free vegetarian feast each Wednesday night at the Episcopal campus
ministry on the edge of UNCG. He went the following Wednesday only to
find hungry college students and homeless persons who showed no interest in the spiritual nourishment afterward. But Fred stayed and absorbed
the Hindu philosophy class, captivated by people who were ready and willing to talk genuinely about theology and their own faith journeys. After

the talk, he cornered the young Hindu monks dressed in saffron-colored robes and asked them everything he could think of about their beliefs, scripture study, meditation, and austere spiritual practices.

Fred felt energized by this encounter, and he felt that God was within reach. After a night of food and fellowship, he walked to a nearby used bookstore and bought copies of the *Bhagavad Gita* and the second canto of the *Srimad Bhagavatam*, two primary volumes of Hindu scripture. He spent hours absorbing the riveting theology, which was nothing like what he had experienced in the Christian church.

Fred returned regularly for the Wednesday night feasts the Hindus called *prasad*. Fred learned that, for Hindus, food was an essential aspect of spiritual practice. *Prasad* was considered consecrated and holy—like Communion—and these meals were Hindus' social justice; feeding people spiritual food was their evangelism.

The Hindu devotees invited Fred to the local temples and home gatherings in neighboring communities. He found no disingenuous pilgrims—only those in steadfast movement toward the Divine. The Hindus' hospitality and sincere practices, combined with Fred's thirst for the sacred, was the formula for his continued momentum along the Eastern paradigm.

✝ ॐ ✝ ॐ ✝ ॐ ✝ ॐ ✝ ॐ ✝ ॐ ✝ ॐ ✝ ॐ ✝ ॐ ✝ ॐ ✝ ॐ ✝

Years after the first Sunday I worshiped at First Baptist Church, I awoke to the realization that I was a member of an evangelical denomination. Then I discovered that I was the only Southern Baptist in the history of America who seemed to have skipped church on the day they handed out the spiritual gift of evangelism.

One Sunday afternoon, about fifty adults and a handful of teens sat at long tables in the fellowship hall and voluntarily took a spiritual gift assessment. I scored through the roof on encouragement and mercy but then had to cover my remedial evangelism scores under sweaty palms. I realized that I would have made a faithful member of some other Christian denomination that was not hustling Jesus at every turn.

Yet I loved the tenets of the Southern Baptist Church: scripture study, religious freedom that kept faith between God and the individual, sacred hymns, fine fellowship, and an ecclesiology that kept decision making at the local church level. But I felt like a disappointment to my Southern Baptist family when it actually came to sharing the gospel with words. Jesus was my Savior, but I never felt comfortable imposing him on others. I saw the invitation to Christ as a path filled with acts of service and love. Banging Bibles over sullen heads was not my bag; feeding people, hugging people, and loving people was.

Because most Southern Baptists tend to have one natural evangelical gift or two, disinterest in preaching the gospel with words created internal struggle and guilt for me. My growing spiritual struggles coincided with First Baptist's continued encouragement for my apparent gifts for ministry—gifts that I didn't recognize in myself as existing. Questions and tensions of evangelicalism, diversity, gender roles, and cultural sensitivity brewed within me. I was absorbed in my struggles, and I didn't see myself as ministry material.

But First Baptist saints like Delores, senior pastor Dr. Montgomery, and associate and youth pastor Rev. Delaney didn't see my lack of natural evangelical skills as worrisome. They saw my other budding gifts as equally useful in the kingdom. They invested themselves in my spiritual progress; at each step of my adolescence, they nudged me along with as much care and love as my own mother provided.

Dr. Montgomery and Rev. Delaney recruited me to preach Youth Sunday sermons, sit on churchwide committees, and participate in worship leadership. These two ministers were more progressive than typical Baptist clergymen in the South; they confidently rooted themselves in strong academic traditions, intense biblical study, and sound-minded gender politics. Still, the precepts of my denomination left me with the sense that female ordained leadership in the Southern Baptist Church was an anomaly. Women could never be full-time professional church leaders—especially a Southern Baptist woman with no gift for evangelism.

When I entered Salem College, the oldest women's college in the United States, I carried this faith struggle with me, yet I imagined that the Southern Baptist principles of my middle school and high school years were indestructible. Still, I found my conservative Christianity waning under the tutelage of professors who strove to empower the young women in their care.

My Baptist upbringing didn't leave much room for other denominations, or God forbid, other religions. Each Salem College candidate for the Bachelor of Arts degree was required to take a religion or philosophy course; neither of which held academic interest for me. But my reluctance to take one course—philosophy—outweighed my reluctance for the other, so I opted for an Eastern religious traditions course.

Eastern Religious Traditions was taught by a Mennonite professor who lectured barefoot and wore a tiny, black earring. He led the course through the lens of key texts, including the *Dhammapada*, the *Tao De Ching*, and the *Bhagavad Gita*. For the first time in my life, I realized that the spiritual world was much bigger than the Christian spheres to which I belonged.

I found the Eastern texts to be as real and inspiring as the Bible. I resonated with the *Bhagavad Gita,* the ancient text depicting God in the form of a chariot driver named Krishna who counseled the warrior Arjuna. I had no sense that Krishna was any different from Jesus. Krishna was as personal and accessible as Christ had been when I ran my hands across the rough bricks of the First Baptist Church sanctuary.

✝ ॐ ✝ ॐ ✝ ॐ ✝ ॐ ✝ ॐ ✝ ॐ ✝ ॐ ✝ ॐ ✝ ॐ ✝ ॐ ✝ ॐ ✝

I remained steadfast in my academic pursuits at Salem without much regard to spiritual nourishment. I pursued a pre-law curriculum and majored in history, added another major of French, and prepared for life after undergraduate studies.

Though the Eastern traditions course had energized me, I had no intention of taking another religion class. I fulfilled my degree's requirement and focused on future ambitions propelled by my childhood financial struggles: law school, money, power, and prestige.

I spent college summers at home working and attending First Baptist Church, which I had neglected most of the school year. Pastors and parishioners welcomed me back as if I'd never left. I was twelve years old again, and Delores Kinston was as happy to see me as an adult as she was when I was a sixth grader sitting across from her at "Mac-Donald's." But she and the First Baptist Church elders who had shepherded me had one pressing question: "Are you *sure* you want to be an attorney?" They didn't disguise their disappointment that I wasn't pursuing a path more suited to the spiritual gifts they saw in me. I couldn't comprehend their distress.

I had been drawn to spirituality my entire life, but I never imagined being so faithful that I would make it my life's work. I saw my Christian walk as one that was never good enough. And growing up financially insecure pushed me toward an occupation I knew would allow me to support my mother and myself. But the mother and church that raised me knew otherwise. I was not called to be an attorney; my life, it seemed, was destined for something else.

In a clever attempt to sway my professional direction, my mother suggested I visit Duke Divinity School while on break for the summer. I was convinced she had lost her mind. But she pushed and pushed, and I finally relented.

"It's Duke University, Dana. You *love* Duke. Our family loves Duke. Your brother went to Duke. Wouldn't you like to go to Duke too?"

My mother convinced me to visit Duke Divinity School later that summer on an official Admissions Day full of scheduled sessions designed to give prospective applicants the best sense of academics and community.

At that time, Rev. Donna Claycomb Sokol, a female United Methodist minister in her early thirties, was Director of Admissions. Donna was a tall, ebullient Democrat with whom I connected immediately due to our mutual love of political campaigns. I was captivated by her intelligence and gregarious energy. I hadn't imagined ministers came in this flavor; the preachers I knew were middle-aged white men in gray suits with leather bound King James Bibles tucked under their armpits.

But Donna wasn't a hologram; she was a real-life, flesh-and-blood charismatic pastor, filled with Holy Spirit fire and grounded in the Biblical text and theology. Her warmth was amplified by the host of angels that surrounded her: Duke Divinity School's faculty, staff, and students who so lovingly extended the arms of Christian hospitality.

I shared my Duke Divinity School visit with the First Baptist Church pastors. They nodded with approval and a wink of "I told you so," even though Duke was not a Southern Baptist seminary.

I moved forward with their support but kept a cautiously optimistic attitude. I hadn't received a fancy, gold-leaf invitation from God calling me to ministry. But I did begin attending First Baptist rigorously again and with the same enthusiasm I had as a teenager. Dr. Montgomery and I discussed my divinity school application. He showed no concern that I hadn't expressed a call to ministry or that I had no formal, collegiate religious education. He was convinced that the gifts he saw spoke for themselves.

I worshiped one last Sunday at First Baptist before I returned to Salem to complete my senior year and French and history degrees. That morning in worship, we belted out the Daniel Schutte invitational hymn written the year I was born, "Here I Am, Lord."

I'd sung this hymn a million times; it had never moved my less-than evangelical self. I only sang it with gusto because of its grammatically correct usage of *whom*.

But the grammar was less important that day; I listened to the words as if hearing them for the first time.

"Whom shall I seeeeeeeend?" Rural North Carolinians drew out the last syllable, long and purposeful. And on that day, the answer gripped me like electricity.

The hymn's words vibrated in my bones, which were now controlled by an energy pulling them down the center aisle. I treaded the golden carpet beneath me, slowly, cautiously, as if I didn't know where I was headed. I landed at the Communion table and a smiling Dr. Montgomery, who opened his arms to greet me. His tall frame bent toward mine, and he lent me his ear. I didn't know what I was going to say, until it came out.

"I feel called to ministry," I whispered, shocked at my own words, like I was speaking in tongues.

"I'm *so* proud of you," he beamed back.

He and First Baptist Church's shepherds had been waiting for this moment since my mother and I crossed the sanctuary threshold when I was eleven. Dr. Montgomery and I stood there together in front of two hundred pilgrims who smiled and seemed to know what was going on, as if I had shouted instead of whispered my calling. They finished their hymn. Tears filled my eyes. When the room fell silent, Dr. Montgomery gave the announcement.

"Our own Dana Trent feels called to the ministry of the gospel of Jesus Christ. She is in the process of applying to Duke Divinity School."

Congregants clapped their hands together and released "Praise Jesus" sighs. Their little girl, whom they nurtured from Southern Baptist faith infancy, finally realized she was no lawyer.

But I hadn't had this revelation on my own. The circuitous path that led to this Holy Spirit moment with Dr. Montgomery at the Communion table was lined with those who mirrored my spirituality to me. Their examples, teachings, and insistence that I had gifts for ministry were the equivalent of someone holding up the looking glass at each juncture to demand, "Don't you see what we see?"

The love of these saints inched me along a journey I didn't even realize I was taking. It's not that law school would have been a bad choice, but it wasn't my truest, deepest calling; and they knew that, even when I did not. Their consistent care reflected a love that wanted more for me than pursuing a life path that I thought would solve my childhood poverty baggage and feelings of inadequacy. Had it not been for the urging of these spiritual guides, I would have had missed the opportunities and growth that would come later—gifts of presence and time to share Christ's love with others.

✝ ॐ ✝ ॐ ✝ ॐ ✝ ॐ ✝ ॐ ✝ ॐ ✝ ॐ ✝ ॐ ✝ ॐ ✝ ॐ ✝ ॐ ✝

After our first successful Hindu encounter at Alice and Mike's, Fred and I became serious in our public commitment among our faith communities. When we attended subsequent Hindu worship services and events, Fred introduced me as his "ordained Southern Baptist minister girlfriend." In spite of his sour exposure to the Christian church and my failed attempt at an interfaith understanding of his baptism, he was unequivocally proud of my pastoral identity.

Fred took pleasure in the introduction rolling off his tongue and Hindu devotees responding with puzzled, sometimes troubled, looks. Suspicion and gentle inquisition usually followed, and Hindus wanted to know how a Southern Baptist minister could sit through two hours of deity worship and not respond with a hellfire and brimstone sermon on the dangers of idolatry. The conservative stereotype of my vocational label did not match my theological disposition. I was a paradox that could not be solved.

But I remembered how I'd obnoxiously pushed for Fred's Christian baptism, and I felt ashamed. Fred still saw me as different from any Christians he'd met, but the pedestal he placed me on was unsubstantiated. I waited for the bottom to crumble beneath me; I didn't feel worthy of his admiration that I was a proper Christian who truly lived the gospel. He didn't know the extent of my struggles, the push-pull of a Christian in-between: too progressive for my Southern Baptist roots and so liberal that I had lost the crux of the message.

When he touted my title, my mind rehearsed unpleasant scenarios I imagined devotees had experienced with Christians like me, including those who'd been scarred by evangelical encounters.

I was sure someone would say, "Oh, I know all about *your* type. You Christians have all told me how fast my Hindu train ride will be to hell!"

Then I'd have to repent in dust and ashes for all the misguided Christians I represented in this moment, when I really wanted to crawl in a hole and disappear. These were the same struggles I'd wrestled with since I was eighteen, left my rural hometown First Baptist Church for college, and discovered that most of America has some brand of Christian baggage.

† ॐ † ॐ † ॐ † ॐ † ॐ † ॐ † ॐ † ॐ † ॐ † ॐ † ॐ † ॐ †

My public profession of a call to ministry was followed by my acceptance to Duke Divinity School and a suggestion of ordination from Dr. Montgomery, who was about to enter retirement, and from First Baptist Church. Before Dr. Montgomery's departure, he was eager to bestow upon me the gift of ordination—a setting apart for gospel ministry. Any heat he'd receive from our denomination over the ordination of a female Southern Baptist minister would be null and void; he'd be enjoying retirement, and I'd be off to divinity school. Dr. Montgomery led the way down the path of ordination, and I walked timidly beside him, trusting our next steps.

By some holy miracle, I passed the First Baptist Church ordination council's approval and stood before the congregation for a vote. Dr. Montgomery anticipated the vote to be a struggle, but I was so naïve about

Southern Baptist politics, I didn't realize how hurtful it could have been. My ordination passed with over ninety percent approval, which was a testimony to First Baptist's love, faith, and support, as well as to the beloved Baptist principle of local church autonomy.

On November 17, 2002, I knelt before the congregation I loved so dearly and vowed to be a faithful minister of the gospel of Jesus Christ. I was twenty-one-year-old college senior with no formal theological education who doubted my spiritual gifts. But the community believed in me, and they trusted the Holy Spirit to prepare me for the ministry experiences to come.

✝ ৯ ✝ ৯ ✝ ৯ ✝ ৯ ✝ ৯ ✝ ৯ ✝ ৯ ✝ ৯ ✝ ৯ ✝ ৯ ✝ ৯ ✝ ৯ ✝

I carried my ordination certificate and my moving boxes to Durham, North Carolina, where I matriculated into Duke Divinity School the fall after graduating from Salem College.

Had I known what I was getting myself into, I would have run to the closest public university law school, earned a J. D., and called it a day. At Duke Divinity School, I was an ordained Southern Baptist woman thrown into the Christian theological mix with brilliant religious studies students from Princeton, Wheaton, Yale, Harvard, and other top-name schools. Duke's shining students and famous faculty were more exceptional than I could have imagined.

I realized quickly that rigorous academics were only one part of the divinity school picture. I had been attracted to Duke's community spirit, and the same spirit that exuded from Donna Claycomb Sokol extended to the Department of Student Life and to the Dean of Students who ran a pre-orientation program introducing first-years to Durham's history of social and racial tensions, community divisions, and ministries that sought to bridge the gap. The students in the program became my closest friends.

But newfound friends and endless hours of academic work couldn't keep me from encountering self-doubt and loneliness. While everyone was rambling off fancy theological terms, I felt clunky and uninformed, as if I were raised in an archaic faith that hadn't yet discovered indoor plumbing. I was drowning in Duke's academics and isolation.

On a Tuesday evening in late September, when the weight of academics and theology led me to believe I wasn't equipped to balance it all, I left. I got in my car and drove home with no intention of returning. When I arrived, I collapsed into my mother's arms, longing for the familiarity of something that wasn't challenging my beliefs or draining my brain.

"I can't go back!" I said between desperate tears.

"You need rest and love," she responded, not giving into my all-or-nothing thinking.

She tucked me into the twin bed I'd had since I was five, and I was content to withdraw from Duke the next day. But I woke up in the middle of the night with an intense anxiety and urgency for guidance. I shuffled down the carpeted stairs and sat in my mother's rocking chair. Then I did something I hadn't done since I'd entered seminary: I read the Bible—for devotional purposes, not for an exegetical essay. I have no recollection of what I read. I only remember that my reading was halted by a clear, firm voice coming from our dark apartment living room.

"You have to go back. You *have* to."

The voice didn't sound like the frequently worried, high-pitched angst of my own consciousness. It came from a place outside of me, from within the walls of the home of my youth, a sacred force that seemed to know me. I felt an overwhelming sense of obedience to the voice. I closed the Bible, breathed deeply, and reconciled that I would return to Duke tomorrow, just as the voice had declared. That night, I slept soundly.

I drove back to Durham the next morning, committed to the decision I made the night before. Three years later, by some miracle, I graduated with a Master of Divinity degree from Duke University.

† ✿ † ✿ † ✿ † ✿ † ✿ † ✿ † ✿ † ✿ † ✿ † ✿ † ✿ † ✿ †

The three years at Duke were spent like Jacob wrestling the angel; I survived with a little less than a hip injury.

The Baptist students at Duke were a minority among our United Methodist counterparts. We had our place, and it was under the direction of Dr. Curtis Freeman, director of the Baptist House of Studies. Dr. Freeman nurtured his religious freedom-loving misfits baptized by immersion. He listened to us and guided us as we vented our struggles with our seminary colleagues entangled in orthodox sacramental theology, connectional churches, and complicated ordination processes.

Baptist House personalities rang true to our radical Free Church predecessors. We tended to be immersion elitists who thought ourselves freer and better than our sprinkled Methodist counterparts who consistently had to toe the party line. We were free, but it also meant we lacked internal direction. The women of the Baptist House especially grappled with finding our place in a denomination fifty years behind its time in ordaining and affirming women for ministry. In the end, we secretly envied our United Methodist friends' well-trodden paths.

My divinity school tensions weren't limited to Baptist versus United Methodist ecclesiology; I struggled with myself too. I had been brought up in a "no creed but Christ" experiential faith. My limited exposure to philosophy, doctrine, and orthodoxy made my experience feel inferior. My Duke sisters and brothers were well-versed in liturgy, sacraments, and church polity. I, along with many other Free Church students, had only learned to embrace the fiercely autonomous mantras taught to us by parishes of our youth—as Dr. Freeman so aptly put it, "Ain't nobody gonna tell me what to do but Jesus."

✝ ❧ ✝ ❧ ✝ ❧ ✝ ❧ ✝ ❧ ✝ ❧ ✝ ❧ ✝ ❧ ✝ ❧ ✝ ❧ ✝ ❧ ✝

The same Holy Spirit voice that directed me back to Duke also offered me a community through which I found support during the seminary journey. In an auspicious twist, I was assigned to a field education placement my first year of seminary at Binkley Baptist Church, the beloved parish of my baptism.

The church hadn't changed since I stood in its baptismal waters when I was eleven years old. The congregation was still a rainbow of diversity. Same-sex couples, international visitors, refugees, students, and local university professors of all races and persuasions sat among the now eighty-year-old charter members who envisioned this open, eclectic congregation. The pulpit had remained an instrument of peace and justice and inclusive language.

But the transition back to Binkley while at Duke Divinity School was not without challenges. On weekdays, I studied with high-church, sacramental, orthodox United Methodists who struggled with a denomination that would not ordain openly LGBT persons or bless same-sex unions. On weekends, I served a congregation of extremely progressive, autonomous American Baptists whose chairs were lined with LGBT clergypersons, same-sex partners, and their children. Duke Divinity School was eager to root its students in proper doctrine, tradition, and orthodoxy. Binkley wanted to nurture its Southern Baptist refugees recovering from one too many fundamentalist slaps with a King James Bible. I sympathized with both parties.

Applying scripture and dogma to real persons and their real-life challenges is inherently different from wrestling with creeds in a classroom. Interning at Binkley taught me that on-the-ground ministry requires struggling with large theological questions asked by parishioners who come from complex backgrounds and circumstances. Visiting congregants, teaching children, and administering ministry programming offered me the sacred space to hold church members' stories. The more I traveled with the members of Binkley on their faith journeys of hurts, rejection, and grief, the more I resisted threads of Christianity that fostered exclusion. The intersection of faith and ecclesiology was far from simple.

I found myself in a complicated predicament: I was an ordained Southern Baptist female who was too progressive for her roots, not orthodox enough for Duke Divinity School, and trying to find the balance in Binkley, a congregation so progressive that some outsiders believed it to be Unitarian.

But Binkley preached the gospel in the hard spaces—the disappointments, chaos, and questions of a heterogeneous church community living and serving together. Returning to Binkley Church meant emerging from the shelter of the straightforward, uncomplicated faith of my teens. The religious simplicity of my youth and rigorous Duke Divinity School education amalgamated in a progressive Baptist internship that prepared me for what was to come.

†ॐ†ॐ†ॐ†ॐ†ॐ†ॐ†ॐ†ॐ†ॐ†ॐ†ॐ†ॐ†

The bounds of my spiritual identity were pushed further when I graduated from Duke and enrolled in a one-year Clinical Pastoral Education residency program at the University of North Carolina at Chapel Hill (UNC) Healthcare System.

The Clinical Pastoral Education program at UNC was as rigorous as Duke Divinity School. Under the direction of two veteran supervisors who were experts in their fields, our resident group of six dove intensely into didactics of death, grief, reflective listening, family systems, offering appropriate care, and crisis management. I was assigned to care for the patients receiving palliative care. The resident chaplain who preceded me had earned the title "The Death Chaplain" for his dedicated service to the bedsides of those dying. I would continue in his stead.

One year spent as "The Death Chaplain" was the equivalent of four decades of learning about people, God, and myself. Day after day, I sat with patients and families as crises propelled them into deep faith struggles. My job was to hold the space for yelling, crying, grief, suffering, questioning, and—in very rare moments—celebrating.

I served atheists, conservative and progressive Protestants of all flavors, Catholics, Jews, Pentecostals, strict Jehovah Witnesses, Universalists, Muslims, and every tradition in between. My role, in all instances, was to meet patients and families where they were and offer support based on their needs.

I was trained to say, "Tell me. . . . " and then repeat what I heard. I learned (the hard way) not to answer the question, *Why is this happening?* but instead to make room for all the emotions that accompany these essential human wonderings in times of health crises.

I stood in for Catholic priests who were unable to make it to bedsides of the dying. I baptized interfaith babies of Jewish fathers and Protestant mothers. I imposed ashes on burned-out attending physicians and nurses. I held the hands of drunks and meth addicts after middle-of-the-night public intoxication arrests landed them in the Emergency Department. I listened compassionately to stories of bleeding patients in trauma bays after they'd been stabbed by relatives with kitchen knives. I was called "Pastor" and then "Satan!" in thirty-second intervals by a rapid-cycling bipolar patient who was off her medication. I prayed for the transition of patients younger than myself whose chronic illnesses had finally consumed their fragile forms. I waited with a family whose loved one ended her life by ingesting antifreeze. I attended peaceful cancer deaths and removal of medical support for patients whose bodies were ninety percent burned. I disposed of the cherished motorcycle boots of a patient whose limb was traumatically amputated in a hit-and-run.

In that magical year, I was a witness to individual theological interpretations of life, death, and illness—but not from religious scholars, theologians, or even churchgoers. I met real people, jerked from their daily routines into nightmares of worst-case scenarios, posing the universal *Why?* to a life source they didn't understand. My First Baptist Church, Binkley Baptist Church, and Duke Divinity School paths merged, and the Holy Spirit showed up. My job was not to prattle on about the problem of evil or the brokenness of humanity. Instead, I was taught to make room for anger, questions, sorrow, rage, denial, and peace.

By the end of my chaplain residency year, I had seen nearly two hundred patients die. But death was not what I had expected it to be. The humanity that connected me to the person in the bed meant that I could feel the sacred moment when the spirit left its body. And, for a holy second, I could feel the spirit hovering in the room, offering a last kiss goodbye or brushing a loved one's cheek. Then it was gone. The room was just a hospital room again, sterile and cold, and we were a family and a chaplain sitting next to an empty shell in tears and silence.

When I met patients and families in these moments, no faith perspective seemed obscure. Every journey felt like a whole and loving reverberation of the Sacred.

† ॐ † ॐ † ॐ † ॐ † ॐ † ॐ † ॐ † ॐ † ॐ † ॐ † ॐ †

My path leading to ordination began with a cluelessness that could only have been unfurled by grace. Early exposure to Binkley Baptist Church's diversity and progressive view of ministry was the cinder block beneath my simple, conservative First Baptist faith.

At ordination, I was unaware of how much I didn't know. Each step unfolded before me, and I could have only seen the providence looking back. The tension between conservative and progressive Christianity, the Binkley versus First Baptist faith, propelled me into growth and acceptance of a wider interpretation of God and gospel.

The journey was always made clear by a fellow sojourner: a school friend, pastor, youth leader, teacher, professor, church member, relative, or parent. These pilgrims are known by their collective name: grace.

From Salem College's Eastern Traditions 101 course to hospital patients and families, each glimpse of another faith journey prepared me for a lifetime with a Hindu monk—a priest named *Gauravani das*.

✝ॐ✝ॐ✝ॐ✝ॐ✝ॐ✝ॐ✝ॐ✝ॐ✝ॐ✝ॐ✝ॐ✝

I never pressed Fred for details as to why he left the monastery. Asking could have done two things: if his time at Audarya had ended badly, it would have been uncomfortable to discuss. Or if it had been a cherished time, it would have given Fred opportunity for sentimentality—a dangerous path that may have bred a longing to return. After all, five years of your twenties spent living as a monk is practically a lifetime; I worried that he'd want to see his investment through.

One Saturday night after a dinner date, Fred had an idea. "Why don't I show you photos from the monastery?"

"Um. OK. Sure." Realizing I sounded less than supportive, I mustered up the enthusiasm to say, "I'd love to see your photos."

Fred pulled a shoebox from his closet and removed the lid. We sat on the floor of his one-bedroom apartment and examined the photos one by one. He considered each snapshot carefully before handing it to me. I studied his face for signs of regret, anger, or longing.

The first photograph was of a slender young man in a white robe with a shaved head and wire-framed glasses. He was leaning against a wall and holding a glass of water. I could feel his loneliness through the glossy photo paper. The image captured the personal struggles monastics face while looking deep at themselves and who they are in relation to God.

I recognized the young man in the photo as *Gauravani das*, Fred's Hindu name. But the sad, thin, and vulnerable twenty-something didn't bear much resemblance to the robust man that sat before me.

"It's time," he said, while I stared at the picture with a broken heart. "Time for what?" I asked, startled. *Time to go back? Time to break up?* "Time to tell you everything."

✝ ॐ ✝ ॐ ✝ ॐ ✝ ॐ ✝ ॐ ✝ ॐ ✝ ॐ ✝ ॐ ✝ ॐ ✝ ॐ ✝ ॐ ✝

His senior year of college, Fred became a regular attendee at the Wednesday night Hindu feasts and other community activities. He became a full-fledged vegetarian, nonsmoker, and practitioner of yoga and meditation. Each day he gravitated more toward Hindu rituals and deep philosophical scripture. As he approached his college graduation, he looked for ways to incorporate his faith into life after school—and secretly daydreamed of cooking in a monastery.

Fred's family was aware of his religious path but not entirely enthusiastic. He revealed small bits of his beliefs at a time as he sensed his family's growing anxiety of what he would do after he completed his degree.

Fred once tried to explain chanting to a family member at dinner.

"It goes like this," he said. "*Hare Krishna, Hare Krishna, Krishna, Krishna, Hare Hare. Hare Rama, Hare Rama, Rama Rama, Hare Hare.*"

The family member responded in a gruff Southern voice, "Why you gotta say Harry so many times, honey?"

The Eastern paradigm was a far cry from the Christian tradition of his youth. It was difficult for Fred's family—and even college friends—to grasp and accept his growing affection for the Eastern tradition. Hinduism was foreign and unknown. Being a Hindu in the Bible Belt seemed as strange as a middle-aged man wearing footed pajamas to the grocery store. Fred knew that if he wanted to grow in his practice, he'd have to find an environment where it was welcome and acceptable.

After graduation, Fred took a leap; he traveled to two urban Hindu temples in Kansas and Florida to experience a fully functioning Gaudiya Vaishnava community with daily deity worship and rituals. Up to that point, he had only attended Hindu feasts at the Episcopal Center and small home gatherings.

The Kansas and Florida temples were grand and opulent. Fred followed their schedules: waking each day to pray at 4:00 a.m., worshiping throughout the day, and washing the temple floors in the afternoon as an offering of service. He loved the quiet afternoon work. He felt like he was serving God—making God's house clean and welcoming. In the evenings he attended *Bhagavad Gita* classes. But Fred struggled when he wasn't praying or scrubbing floors. The temple was open to the public, and it received hundreds of visitors each day for worship. Large crowds gathered during services. Hindu devotees squeezed in and out of the sacred space, and the lack of quiet and personal time suffocated him.

Fred longed for sustained silence for practice and service and determined he may be more suited to a monastic environment. He returned to North Carolina and accepted an invitation to offer technology services at Bhaktivedanta Archives in a quiet, rural Gaudiya Vaishnava community in the center of the state. There he lived as a monk, engaging in early morning and evening worship, contemplative practice, and hours of silence, all while offering IT services during the day. This was where he first encountered his *guru*, Swami Bhakti Vedanta Tripurari.

Swami Tripurari was a student of both Srila B. R. Sridar Maharaja and Srila A. C. Bhaktivedanta Prabhupada, the Indian monk and priest responsible for bringing the Gaudiya Vaishnava tradition of Hinduism to the West. Swami had been a practitioner of the tradition for four decades; he'd lived as a monk since age twenty-five.

Swami was visiting the North Carolina Gaudiya Vaishnava community when Fred first heard him preach. At their initial encounter, Fred was overwhelmed by Swami's spiritual knowledge. Fred felt Swami had truly experienced the Divine because he radiated spiritual affection and was so willing to share it with others.

And that's when Fred knew that Swami would be his *guru*.

The remaining piece of his Hindu journey—guidance of a spiritual master—stood before Fred. The integral elements of his ideal Hindu practice were coming together: quiet monasticism, practice, service, and, finally, a *guru*.

After the visit, Fred wrote to Swami and told him how much his heart had resonated with the *guru's* preaching and presence. They exchanged messages, and Fred declared Swami his *guru*. When he sought his spiritual master's first piece of advice, Swami responded, "Wherever you find God consciousness, go there."

Swami invited Fred to serve and study at Audarya monastery in northern California. Fred went earnestly, eager to immerse himself in the quiet monastic experience he longed for. A month after arriving, Fred took first and second initiation from Swami, the equivalent of baptism and ordination into the Hindu priesthood.

Fred was given a new name: *Gauravani das*, or *servant of the teachings of Mahaprabhu*. *Mahaprabhu* is a form of Lord Krishna, whom Gaudiya Vaishnavas consider to be the Supreme Personality of God. Fred served as Audarya's *pujari* (ordained priest) for one-and-a-half years, presiding over morning and evening worship. He arose each morning at 4:00 a.m. to pick flowers for the altar and prepare the deities for the 5:00 a.m. *arati* (worship) service. During the day, Fred cooked for the deities, offered them food, and performed *puja* (worship). He learned the intricacies of the mantras and the moves of each service, which were as complex as a high holy mass in any Catholic cathedral.

Deity worship is an ancient, intricate, scripture-based practice that is the most important work of the monastery and is the focus of temple life. Scripture and philosophy enriched Fred's practice; the deity worship energized and centered him.

But a year-and-a-half of living as a full-time monk and priest in a secluded monastery in northern California was more strenuous than Fred anticipated. When he wasn't caring for the deities, he worked on IT projects for the ministry. Audarya Monastery is a twenty-acre farm with a small crew—monks coming and going but much work still to be done, no matter how small the team. The schedule was intense, and Fred eventually suffered from insomnia and anxiety. Living and serving at Audarya, even in the presence of God and his *guru*, was taxing. He was twenty-seven and didn't feel emotionally mature enough to balance cloistered life and its responsibilities.

Hindus believe that the closer one gets to God, the further away the seeker actually feels. The more Fred approached the infinite, the more he felt his finite nature become apparent.

I was surprised by the reason that Fred left the monastery. I was expecting a dramatic plotline including big blowouts between Swami or the other monks or a rejection of Hinduism altogether. But the reason was simple: Fred wasn't suited to full-time cloistered life. The monastic rhythm, for all its benefits, was difficult.

As an outsider, I always believed that monks and nuns had conquered what the rest of us haven't in our frenzied lives. But even a life entirely focused on God is based, at least for now, in this complicated material world. Monastic life, then, still comes with the standard-issue struggles of our own personal messiness.

✝ ॐ ✝ ॐ ✝ ॐ ✝ ॐ ✝ ॐ ✝ ॐ ✝ ॐ ✝ ॐ ✝ ॐ ✝ ॐ ✝ ॐ ✝

After eight months of dating, Fred and I visited a local jeweler to look at engagement rings. It was simultaneously one of the most intense and delightful moments of my life. Glass cases stretched as far as the eye could see, full of shiny baubles and sparkling radiance.

In his practicality, Fred wanted an engagement ring that was simple, round, and low because women's rings that towered two inches from their skinny fingers scratched arms and got caught in sweaters. We chose a unique design we both liked, with diamonds and sapphires that reminded Fred of Lord Krishna's blue skin.

As I eagerly anticipated our wedding day, Fred reminded me that he hadn't even proposed yet.

"I'm not sure when this will happen. It will probably be well into next year, maybe even the year after that."

I tried to keep my composure, but it was all I could do to hold in my frustration. I walked away from the jewelry store in a huff dramatic enough to let him know I was angry.

Rationally, I believed Fred when he said it would be a while. But I hoped he would change his mind, be desperate to marry me, live with me, and get started on life happily every after much sooner than "the year after next."

I'll give him three years of dating, tops, I thought to ease my hurt feelings. We'd only been dating eight months, but I was offended by his timetable, and I didn't want to be like the women you read about in magazines who've given boyfriends the best fifteen years of their lives.

But I only waited three more months.

The day after Thanksgiving, we rented *The Proposal*—not on purpose—because I'm a lifelong Betty White fan. Before we began the movie, Fred rummaged around in his closet on his knees.

"What are you doing?" I asked, annoyed.

"Nothing." Fred sounded mischievous.

"Hurry up!"

Still on his knees, Fred turned around quickly, looked at me, and scooted over to where I was sitting. He pulled the ring from behind his back and opened the box.

"Will you marry me?" he asked sincerely and vulnerably, as if I might say no.

"Is it *real*?" I replied. Yes, those were the first words to come out of my mouth—the worst possible response you could give a man on his knees asking to spend the rest of his life with you.

"Oh my God, I mean, yes! Yes! Of course! Yes!" I recovered, squealed, cried, hugged, and kissed him all at the same time.

Fred teased me about "Is it *real*?" for thirty minutes until I was given a chance to explain myself.

"You'd been so adamant about the timeline. I thought for sure you were teasing me with a fake proposal."

"Is it *real*?" Fred mimicked back, in my high-pitched nervous voice.

I would never, ever live that down.

CHAPTER

WADING INTO MARRIED LIFE

Where you go, I will go; where you lodge, I will lodge;
your people shall be my people, and your God my God.

Ruth 1:16, NRSV

Fred and I announced our engagement to family and friends, including a retelling of my embarrassing *Is it* real? response. When we told our faith communities, they met us with shouts of curiosity, excitement, and wonder. Thankfully, no one made sour faces and said, "This is a very, very bad idea."

Even though our duo was only half-Messianic, Fred and I thought it prudent to enter into the age-old Christian ritual of premarital counseling. All marriages have challenges, yes, but ours would begin with the added layer of slowly merging two very different faith traditions. Binkley Baptist Church's Associate Pastor, the Rev. W. Dale Osborne, agreed to officiate our wedding and help us think through the complexity of our soon-to-be interfaith married life.

Fred and I had no fewer than five sessions with Dale over the course of six months, all sprinkled with his pastoral patience. At the first two sessions, we sat together politely on the couch in Dale's office, offering common courtesies like Southern couples from my grandmother's era. We were still in the honeymoon phase of dating; we lived in separate towns and hardly ever fought. Any data we had on each other's personalities, faith, and tendencies was gathered in bite-sized pieces on weekend dates and weeknight conversations.

During the sessions, I described my Christianity as inferior to Fred's Eastern profundity. This was nothing new to my faith walk; I'd spent most of my life and spiritual journey comparing myself to others. I hadn't afforded myself the grace to be just me, the fledgling Christian who often felt lost and socially awkward. Dale immediately sensed the tension surrounding the topic of philosophical depth.

Fred had experienced a life-giving revelation in Eastern philosophy, and he longed for the same for me. He wanted me to dig into Christian philosophy—headfirst, propelling myself into a deeper, more integrated walk with Christ. This made me feel even more like a Christian flunky. The three of us discussed prayer, and I mentioned that I wanted Fred to join me in my method of prayer, just as I was giving chanting a chance.

"Remember to value each tradition equally. One framework is not more advanced than the other," Dale offered.

These words were comforting, but I doubted my ability to believe. My tendency toward Christian inferiority would be one of our most strenuous interfaith marriage challenges.

"I want you both to remember that spirituality is what drew you together in the first place." My mind flashed to checking eHarmony boxes on a cold Saturday. "And it's what will keep you together," Dale finished.

Focusing on the theological aspect of my connection with Fred—with all our emotional baggage in tow—would require work. Dale's gentle instructions reminded us that any marriage—but especially a Christian-Hindu interfaith partnership—needed consistent nurturing and communication. Fred and I would have to meet at the well constantly, drawing on the sacred water that excited us in the weeks following our first date.

In my fantasy, I had imagined a perfect balance of the best of our Christian and Hindu traditions, like if Mother Teresa married Gandhi. I took it for granted that Fred and I would always be enthralled with each other and one another's religions. I had forgotten that the moon waxes and wanes, tides ebb and flow, and that faith—and people—are not static.

✝ॐ✝ॐ✝ॐ✝ॐ✝ॐ✝ॐ✝ॐ✝ॐ✝ॐ✝ॐ✝ॐ✝

Fred and I married on July 17, 2010, at Binkley Baptist Church in Chapel Hill. We hosted an environmentally-friendly wedding on a limited budget with endless support from our families, friends, and the Binkley community. Our ceremony was decidedly Christian; we long had given up the dream of a fancy, expensive Indian wedding with elephants and a fire sacrifice. Fred's *guru* didn't officiate weddings, so Fred was content for Dale to serve as our mutual clergyperson, with Fred's Hindu godbrother and godsister representing the Eastern aspect of his life. We incorporated a Sanskrit version of the Lord's Prayer, but otherwise, it was a Christian affair, knowing the Hindu counterpart would arrive soon after: the Indian ashram honeymoon.

After the wedding, Fred and I moved into a one-bedroom apartment. I hadn't shared a home with a man since my mother and I left my father in our Indiana trailer when I was six years old. My brother is also eighteen years my senior, so I hadn't learned the routines of men, let alone those of a former Hindu monk.

Fred's deep-seated Eastern values reflected his aversion to materialism in the home. His disdain for fancy accoutrements—or even mediocre ones—meant that we furnished our 875 square feet with hand-me-downs and thrift store decor.

To his credit, Fred doesn't buy anything unless he has to. He has no desire for society's version of the American Dream. He doesn't long for adult furniture, an SUV, or a home with a two-car garage. He'd rather sit on the floor, walk to work, and build a tiny, sustainable cabin. If Fred had his way, we'd still share the barely twin-sized bed he inherited from a friend when he returned from the monastery. The rusted filing cabinet with no drawers would be our end table. The questionable red couch from a university dormitory he scavenged from a thrift store would anchor our living room. And, if I hadn't insisted on its disposal, our guests would sit a spell on the mildewed, jungle-themed love seat that (barely) survived an apartment flood.

Fred drives a scratched-up, dented Mitsubishi with three missing hubcaps that smells like someone left a bacon biscuit in the backseat during the Carter administration. He calls the missing wheel covers and pork air freshener his "theft-deterrent mechanism." I call it absurd. One of the few times I drove *The Baconator*, a man flagged me down at a gas station and begged to buy the last hubcap. I should have given it to him.

By Western standards, Fred had long since accomplished the lifelong Eastern practitioner's task of quieting material desires. I went to seminary with holy persons like this who lived a similar Christian theology of economics. They dove in dumpsters and held community potlucks for the poor. They were mindful of what they consumed. I admired their practices but never had the courage (or desire) to implement them in my own life—until I had a Hindu roommate.

After we married, I recognized that Fred's Hindu economics had *theological* value. He inspired me to lessen my penchant for purchasing junk just to fill a space. The newfound lifestyle led to greater peace—and it provided opportunity for us to be more intentional in our own giving. When a friend needed assistance with making ends meet, we could help. When there were urgent needs at monasteries, nonprofits, and the faith communities we attended, we could assist. Those moments brought more joy than a fancy couch and *As seen on TV!* gadgets.

Still, like most American kids I grew up with what one of my relatives refers to as "the idiot box." But because of the strict enforcement of my mother, I watched a lot of CNN and weekly dramas with moral messages. But during the summer after seventh grade while visiting my paternal grandparents in Indiana, I developed an addiction to *The Young and the Restless* that I didn't tell my mother about until I was in college. By then, she'd begun watching it too.

I also lived for watching baseball on TV, a pastime that I shared with my father. I fought my mother for control of the remote after supper and soaked up the glories of bat cracks and smooth-voiced commentators. Baseball drew a sacred line from North Carolina to Indiana, connecting me with the man I barely knew.

Fred didn't have addictions to soap operas or baseball; he hadn't lived with a TV since he graduated from college and became a monk. Even when he returned to secular life, he'd never reinstituted the habit of wasted hours. I had heard of these people; I didn't trust them.

But TV was another compromise in the long list of what it would take to balance my Western habits with a former Hindu monk. We were married several months before I realized how the idiot box had affected my life. First, it had been addictive—save an evening for this program, can't miss that episode. Second, it was mindless—a post-work unwind easily turned into hours gone and time wasted. Third, it was consumptive—it poisoned my body with symptoms of wanting to taste the latest thing and try the hottest trend that would, supposedly, improve my life.

Since surviving TV separation I now strongly advocate for TV-free households. My evenings went from sitcom marathons to lively conversations with my husband, cooking, walking, writing, and reading. I got more accomplished in the sixteen hours I was conscious than I ever had in my life (why hadn't I thought of this in graduate school?), and our interfaith marriage was the direct beneficiary of these good habits. Had we kept the TV, we may not have kept talking when interfaith struggles surfaced as sarcasm, resentment, and fights. The TV would have been an instant numbing device, a catchall with a power button that zapped the energy needed to navigate the first years of a Christian-Hindu marriage.

✝ ॐ ✝ ॐ ✝ ॐ ✝ ॐ ✝ ॐ ✝ ॐ ✝ ॐ ✝ ॐ ✝ ॐ ✝ ॐ ✝ ॐ ✝

The push-pull of our first year of living together was also challenged by balancing Fred's introversion and my extroversion. Introverts are a careful species, quiet and thoughtful, usually content to be alone. While I learned when he needed his own space, he learned when I needed him to listen to me verbalize a problem in order to uncover the solution. He had to be willing to be social, attend parties, and talk with people at church. I had to be willing to sit contemplatively in Hindu worship and to tiptoe around the house when he chanted.

Fred's strong introspective nature made him a prime monastic and priest. His gifts of reflection, intuition, and insight were stronger than anyone I'd ever met. But they took getting used to. Through many mistakes, I uncovered what made him comfortable and uncomfortable. At the

81

conclusion of the first year of marriage, I received the highest praise an introvert could offer.

"Being with you is like being by myself," he mumbled one Saturday morning over oatmeal.

"Whaaaaat?" I asked, hurt.

"When I'm with you, I feel as good as when I'm by myself."

Was this a trick? A clever, backhanded compliment? I couldn't process the meaning of his words internally, so I had to talk it through aloud.

"So you're saying that being with me is like being by yourself? But, you love being by yourself, right? So actually, being around me is a good thing?"

"Exactly," he replied as he sipped his coffee from his favorite green mug.

"You're giving me a compliment?"

"Yes," he sighed.

"Oh. OK. Well, then . . . thank you."

This was one of the nicest things my introverted husband could say to me, and I nearly missed it. If having me around was that comfortable, then married life was suiting Fred.

A year in, I found myself creeping toward introversion too. I became more timid in spaces that held large groups and a lot of talking. I learned to quiet my voice of interruption and rebuttal. I learned to listen to others. I learned to listen to God.

✝ ॐ ✝ ॐ ✝ ॐ ✝ ॐ ✝ ॐ ✝ ॐ ✝ ॐ ✝ ॐ ✝ ॐ ✝ ॐ ✝ ॐ ✝

The first year of marriage was a departure from the status quo of my single life. It was a new, magical world of simplicity while we strove to build a foundation that would withstand the interfaith challenges to come.

Fred and I sorted through the small issues of a stinky love seat and long evenings where we were forced to talk to each other instead of stare at a TV. But we knew there would be larger, more complex issues to wrestle with as well. We had to establish a way of life demonstrative of two ordained ministers from two very different traditions living under one roof.

CHAPTER

SABBATH-KEEPING

In whatever way people take refuge in me, I reciprocate with them accordingly.
Everyone in all circumstances . . . follows my path.

Bhagavad Gita: Its Feeling and Philosophy, 4.11

When we were first engaged, Fred and I searched for manuals and websites on navigating Christian-Hindu marriages. It was a futile mission; we didn't find anyone who had written the operating instructions for an east-meets-west romance.

We found tomes on Protestant-Catholic interfaith marriages, articles on famous Jewish-Christian pairings, and a few mentions of Muslim-Christian couples. Most of the interfaith relationship wisdom we encountered encouraged each partner to practice his or her own religious tradition separately with no mixing or sharing of worship. I believed this to be because a plethora of interfaith marriages contain one spouse who is not practicing or not interested in religion, which makes cultivating a solitary faith journey a necessity, not an option.

"Do you think this is the route we should take?" I asked Fred after we read several frustrating accounts on interfaith separation.

"What would we talk about?" His voice revealed concern. Fred loved nothing more than to parse sermons, liturgical experiences, and complex scripture passages. His need for theological discussion could be annoying—sometimes argumentative—but at least he was interested in talking about God.

"True. We'd have separate sabbath experiences. It'd be hard to relate to one another."

Making sabbath-keeping a disconnected affair sounded deceptively easy but also dangerous. Divided worship meant dissociation. Neither one of us would be invested in the other's beliefs, worship, or faith community. We'd be individuals on parallel paths, never to cross. There was a larceny in that choice—something sacred stolen that God had actually intended for us to experience together.

† ॐ † ॐ † ॐ † ॐ † ॐ † ॐ † ॐ † ॐ † ॐ † ॐ † ॐ † ॐ † ॐ †

Formulating and maintaining an active, balanced sabbath-keeping schedule with a devoutly religious partner of an intrinsically different faith is like asking a spatially challenged person to move a wide armchair through a narrow doorway. The victim will try to squeeze the furniture through the doorway as is, struggling and cursing, banging the door frame repeatedly. She determines she will surely have to saw off half of the chair to make it work until some clever person points out that the chair can be turned on its side, tilted, and gently guided over the threshold. The chair hasn't changed; its volume and shape have remained the same, but the perspective has shifted.

Our armchairs were the religious traditions we brought to the marriage. The depth or breadth of neither tradition was lost, but we had to figure out the angle by which we could get it in the living room.

This is not as simple as brokering a deal between a Baptist and a Presbyterian. We're talking about solving a puzzle that has, according to most religious circles, diametrically opposing theological tenets. There was no meeting in the middle with Moses, Abraham, or the Trinity, and no common Resurrection, baptism, or scripture. These were the Mutt and Jeff of religious perspectives.

"Worshiping separately would be easier," I offered, when I had taken the time to consider the consequences of merging traditions that felt as though they were on opposite ends of the God spectrum.

"No," Fred replied adamantly. His intuition told him that choice would be the beginning of the end. We'd stop talking about faith; we'd begin to segregate our other interests, and our life together would be over.

"You sure about this?" I asked, mostly because I wasn't.

"Yep. If we split up our sabbath, we are admitting to God, to each other, and to our friends and family that this was all a hoax and that there was no such thing as an interfaith marriage. We might as well rewind the last three years, be single again, and do our own thing."

I was surprised by his conviction.

"OK, then. We stick together?" I proposed.

"We're stuck."

We shook hands, kissed, and agreed to our own interfaith household golden rule: always worship together.

We brainstormed about a smooth schedule of Christian and Hindu services—equally balanced, equally attended. It was a circus rose solution—a beautiful hybrid of yellow and red flowers, shimmering in our budding garden of interfaith marriage. But we hadn't anticipated droughts, malnourishment, questions, resentment, and imbalance that bore thorns on the stems of even the most heavenly of blooms.

† ॐ † ॐ † ॐ † ॐ † ॐ † ॐ † ॐ † ॐ † ॐ † ॐ † ॐ † ॐ †

I am a linear thinker who gravitates toward organization and order. I imagined these traits would be helpful in establishing a Christian-Hindu sabbath-keeping routine. Once we agreed to attend worship services together, I envisioned a simple sabbath-keeping design, like a child's chore list, carefully hung on the refrigerator with stickers indicating which days to do what. But faith is not linear—neither are human hearts. It turns out that establishing an east-meets-west interfaith sabbath-keeping routine was about as graceful as a baby giraffe learning to walk.

SAFFRON CROSS

My new apartment with Fred was thirty minutes from Binkley Baptist Church, a spiritual home that cultivated my pastoral identity and from which I lived a mere mile and a half away during divinity school and after my graduation. This thirty-minute distance was almost too much to bear; Binkley felt as far away as North Dakota.

"It's *only* thirty minutes away, Dana," the church ladies would chastise me when I whined.

"But I can't pop in and out when I want to. I can't go pray. I can't attend meetings or go to programs during the week." I felt like a lost sheep, crying for a family that felt two thousand miles away—though we were separated only by twenty miles of I-40.

Fred wasn't a member of a local Hindu temple; his church home was wherever Swami was, which at that juncture happened to be monasteries in California, Costa Rica, and western North Carolina.

There were three Hindu temples within miles of our apartment, thanks to an influx of Indians who moved to central North Carolina for its robust job market. We lived in the heart of the Indian neighborhoods, which we hadn't chosen on purpose but was auspicious and appreciated. Vegetarian Indian food and Hindu worship were plentiful, and those are two of Fred's favorite things.

Unlike mainstream Protestantism, lay Hinduism is a religion primarily of the home and festival. Hindu temples have been established in America mainly as a focal point of community and culture away from indigenous lands, rather than for sabbath-keeping urgency. Hinduism is a way of life. At its most devout level, each hour, each meal, each early morning mumble of a chant, and each gesture for the care of deities is infused with Eastern tradition. By virtue of time alone, a faithful Hindu's routine makes even the most pious deacon seem like a pagan.

Hindus don't frantically dress and push kids out the door on Sunday morning for church services. They instead keep altars in their home—their spiritual hubs—as a centering force of God in the house and heart. These altars vary in shapes and sizes from the humble to the opulent. They hold sacred objects in the same way a Christian altar holds the Bible and the Lord's Supper.

Fred insisted we have an altar in our home. I was fine with it, so long as Jesus had as much limelight as the deities and Swami. We used a two-shelf, three-foot tall bookcase we received for our wedding and arranged it in a corner nook of our apartment. Our new altar held an icon of Christ, photos of deities, and a portrait of Swami. Three candles representing the Trinity illuminate the deities' photos. Dried garlands from India lay next to a brass bell and *ghee* lamp used for Hindu food and flower offerings. Volumes of sacred scripture, commentaries, and devotionals from each tradition line the shelves. Prayer beads sit on the edge, begging for time and hands.

✝ॐ✝ॐ✝ॐ✝ॐ✝ॐ✝ॐ✝ॐ✝ॐ✝ॐ✝ॐ✝ॐ✝ॐ✝

"If we're going to attend worship together, how do you propose we do it?"

Fred and I walked briskly around the park's paved trail as leaves fell from the trees. Our evening walks had become a way to decompress after long days, and our conversation usually found its way to theological concerns.

"I dunno. Maybe we alternate Sundays at Binkley and the Balaji temple," Fred replied.

"Maybe."

I already saw cracks in the plan. Binkley's distance squeezed at my heart and at my not-so-stellar church attendance record. I imagined it would get worse; the miles stretched farther and farther. Fred read my mind, a skill he'd acquired when we began living together. He said telepathy was easy with me; I was very predictable.

"Maybe we try finding a progressive church close to the temple." Fred offered.

This was a real, heart-wrenching possibility. Leaving Binkley would be nothing short of painful. But there were loads of churches near the Vaishnava temple, and one of them was bound to match my two requirements of Christian communities: loving Jesus and embracing all persons regardless of gender, race, socioeconomic status, or sexual orientation.

A freshly constructed Episcopal Church around the corner from the Hindu temple fit both tenets. We could attend the early morning Eucharist service at the Episcopal church, then take *darshan* (Sanskrit for *sight* or *seeing* the deity) at the Hindu temple, and our sabbath would be tied up with a nice bow by noon.

When I told the Binkley pastors that Fred and I were going to try this new sabbath permutation, the confession broke my heart. There was no other Binkley, but we had to explore this option.

The first Sunday we visited St. Anne's Episcopal Church, we left our contact information, I took Eucharist while Fred remained in the pew, and we scooted around the corner to our next religious station. When we arrived home and cooked a homemade Indian lunch, a wise-looking fellow rang our apartment doorbell. He announced that he was from St. Anne's and that his wife baked homemade chocolate chip bread to welcome visitors. He refused to come in and sit down, but stood in the doorway as the aroma of rice and *dahl* wafted to his nose.

"Are you Episcopalians?" he inquired with a crisp, Northern accent—a hint that he wasn't from around here.

"Uh, no, sir. I—uh, am—um—a Baptist minister, and my husband is a devout Hindu."

"Oh," he wrinkled his eyebrows, perplexed.

Then, because he was obviously a member of Jesus' holy hospitality crew, his face turned into a giant smile, and he exclaimed, "Well, welcome! Come back soon!" and then he turned to leave.

When we closed the door, I ran to our altar, slumped down to the floor, pressed my hands to my face, and cried.

"What's wrong, my sweet?" Fred put the bread on the kitchen counter and came back over to rub my shoulders.

"He was so kind," I said between sobs.

His Christian hospitality made me ache for Binkley, for the simple days when sabbath was comprised of one religion and worship was less than a mile away.

"Is this going to work?" I asked Fred, and he knew what I wanted to know. Would this new rule and new house of worship and interfaith sabbath-keeping *really* work?

"Be patient, my little grasshopper."

"Perhaps it will work," I sighed. If Christians outside of Binkley's walls were as welcoming, maybe I'd be OK.

We were invited to orientation sessions at St. Anne's. Gatherings were followed by wine and cheese receptions (alcohol—at church! I nearly had a Southern Baptist stroke). The church had no shortage of hospitality.

But this parish was huge—with multiple services, a full ministry staff overflowing with resources, and nuclear families with 2.5 children. I missed Binkley's quirky members of all shapes and sizes, orientations, and background. I longed for its rose-colored cushioned chairs and aging charter members who anchored the melting pot congregation. I yearned for Binkley's attendance and budget struggles and overworked ministry staff. I regretted never fully appreciating my years of living practically in Binkley's backyard.

✝ ॐ ✝ ॐ ✝ ॐ ✝ ॐ ✝ ॐ ✝ ॐ ✝ ॐ ✝ ॐ ✝ ॐ ✝ ॐ ✝ ॐ ✝

Shortly after Fred and I married, Fred's *guru* began visiting North Carolina each April and October. Dubbed the "Swami months" in our interfaith household, these weekends were scheduled to the brim with travel and Gaudiya Vaishnava activities.

Swami's semi-annual visits to North Carolina were what his Hindu students called "nectar." These visits were the sweet patches of life—the concentrated good stuff of the spiritual journey. For Hindus, a *guru* is a miniature God here on Earth who demonstrates to his or her students how to love and serve God. The *guru*'s role is one of mercy because God is merciful enough to show us what to do through a human servant. Protestants have a difficult time with this concept; Baptists, especially, get worked up when anyone tells them how to follow Jesus. But I knew it was important for Fred to take advantage of Swami's proximity. And because I did not want to be the first offender of the "worship together" rule, I wanted to take advantage of Swami's wisdom too.

I participated in the first Swami month eagerly and willingly, happy to see Fred inspired. But I hadn't armored myself for the frustration and resentment the Hindu season would bring—a bitterness whose culprit was not the Eastern tradition itself, Swami, or his students. Rather, it was a blend of disapproval from my usually sweet-natured husband and my own gravitation toward feelings of spiritual inadequacy.

Fred is a good man whose one tragic flaw is his persistence toward spiritual perfection that actually makes him a little edgy. He has high spiritual ideals, a quality that served him well as a monk and priest. But in the secular world, this tendency manifested itself as a critique of his own actions and, ultimately, of mine as well. During the Swami months, I felt like Fred was holding a spotlight to all of my religious shortcomings.

Hinduism, when practiced devoutly, is an intense religion in which all things are sacred and every aspect of life from dawn till dusk flows toward the hub called God. There are no notions of one-hour sabbaths and we're done; Hinduism is a full-on commitment to living a life oriented to devotion. Hindus sit for hours on hard floors meditating, chanting, and focusing on intense exegetical sermons offered by wise *gurus*. Hindus are austere creatures, putting aside material desires, grumbling tummies, and wandering minds to worship God.

Swami's students do this very well because he has modeled the way. His students keep impeccable standards of study, worship, and dietary habits. Fred's monastic training with Swami gripped him, leaving deep imprints on his heart.

And now Fred had married little ol' me, whose constitution is not made for fasting and sitting still in two-hour shifts. My first Swami months were filled with flubs, mistakes, and a lack of reverence that overcame me once I slammed into the one-hour mark of Hinduism. Fred's embarrassment manifested as critical statements and looks that felt like a heavy chain of insults flung at my soul.

Fred's comments stemmed from a near decade of intense study and subsequent monastic training. In order to be a priest at a remote Hindu monastery who rises each morning at 4:00 a.m. to preside over predawn worship, one must have cultivated more spirituality than the average person. Though his comments to me were typically justified, I found it difficult to bear up under the weight of the critical observations he made of me throughout a "Swami month" day: "You're not doing that right! Don't put that music sheet on the ground! Don't point your bare feet at anyone! Don't stand too close to the deities! Don't eat before the food has been offered! Think pure thoughts if you're helping in the kitchen! Don't touch the monks! Don't talk about meat! Wash your hands before you go back for a second helping!'"

Fred's assessments came from a place of devotion, yet I ended up feeling paranoid in the temple setting and constantly fearful of messing up. My inadequacies and Fred's grasping for spiritual idealism were more than enough fuel for our first interfaith fights. A part of me expected Fred to blanket me in compliments of how I was the most tolerant interfaith partner who lovingly made sacrifices to worship with her husband these two months of the year. But instead of compliments, I was constantly receiving critiques. Finally, I cracked.

"This isn't working for me," I said.

"What's not working, Dana?"

"The Swami weekends, Fred. They are not working for me."

Silence. No reaction.

"You think I am not good enough for you, Fred! You think I'm not good enough for the Hindus! I don't know what I'm doing, you always yell at me, and I feel stupid! This just isn't working!"

"What are you saying?"

I kept the silence this time, and the air grew thick between us.

"What do you want me to do?" he asked.

"I dunno. Maybe we need time and space to think this through," I replied, as if the next word to roll off my tongue would begin with *D*, and I didn't mean Dallas.

The conversation ended there, but my internal monologue got worse, as each day shared with Hindus was like surrounding myself with Mother Teresa's clones. Everyone was pious; everyone loved God. Everyone thought of what he or she could do for God before breakfast, while the lone, grumpy Protestant snarled to her husband and Jesus: "You two owe me one!"

In the presence of others on their own spiritual journeys, I always felt like a mess of a Christian. I replayed thoughts of my inconsistent prayer life, lack of daily Bible study, and apathy toward making the sacrifices Jesus calls his followers to make and found these to be my heaviest, most insidious flaws. But worshiping with Hindus brought the perceived inadequacies

I'd carried in Christian circles into bright lights, and I felt like a slug among gilded angels. Swami's students never implied that I was a repellent creature; they never offered me anything but grace and love and hospitality. But worshiping with sojourners who made God the center of their lives was a reminder that I was a me-centered Christian with immature religious tendencies.

So I prayed. When I sat for hours in Hindu worship, I begged Jesus and the deities and all the holy creatures for mercy.

"Mercy," I breathed. "Grace," I repeated.

Nothing happened at first; but over time, I experienced a shift. Deep in my heart, I realized Jesus loved little sluggy me, and he loved me so much that he wouldn't let me stay in this shape forever. He wanted me to grow, and that may have been the reason he introduced me to the Hindus.

As the cycle of Swami months passed, I embraced two rules of survival: one, not to allow Fred's monastic idealism to feed into my own self-loathing and two, that Jesus was bound to be lurking around the Hindu weekends somewhere, I just had to find him. After all, he wasn't banned from Gaudiya Vaishnava functions.

Over time, I learned not to take Fred's appraisals of myself so seriously. I told him to lighten up and tried not to allow his spiritual expectations to change how I felt about myself. I did my best, always showed respect, and sought to learn what I could from each interaction with Hindus. And Jesus always showed up—through a devotee's kind words, Swami's sermons, or shimmering Holy Spirit moments during deity worship. Jesus had been there all along; I just needed to see him.

Our temporary intensity toward Hinduism for two months of the year was a small price to pay for the theological and spiritual wealth Fred experienced through the association with his *guru* and friends. It was worth the by-product I received too, albeit stubbornly.

I began to see Hindu weekends as a time for nourishing my own faith walk. I meditated on Christ *and* Krishna, prayed the Lord's Prayer with my *japa* beads, and learned how universal principles can be applied to both Hinduism and Christianity. Christians paid big money for Christ-centered weekend retreats, and I had been gifted with a whole slew of them—the benefit of marrying a man whose devout faith attracted me to him in the first place.

I just had to tilt the armchair.

† ॐ † ॐ † ॐ † ॐ † ॐ † ॐ † ॐ † ॐ † ॐ † ॐ † ॐ † ॐ †

A year after balancing Swami months and trying to establish some semblance of a Christian-Hindu sabbath-keeping routine close to our apartment, Fred and I were invited to teach two weeks of Sunday school classes for Binkley Church School's Interfaith Encounter Course. It was an invitation back into the fold after I had been so ashamed that I'd left, whined about the drive, and discovered that well-intentioned mega-churches with plenty of resources and members could not hold a candle to my precious, quirky Binkley community.

An invitation to teach Sunday school was the grace-filled gateway Fred and I needed to begin attending again. We had to bear the drive to participate in the course; we were obligated to teach, and even better, we prepared two lectures on Hinduism that generated subsequent interfaith conversations and a post-worship gathering on in-depth topics related to Hindu theology of the soul.

Until we joined Binkley's Interfaith class, Fred had always been a little put off by the Christian aspect of our lives. His preteen baggage of altar calls, salvific formulas, and what he observed to be a troubling disconnect between Christ's teachings and Christians' actions weighed on him. He loved the Binkley ministry staff and the welcome he received from the members, but he longed for deeper interaction with God and scripture when he visited.

Typically the educational programs at Binkley, including the Interfaith Encounter course, were a gathering where theologians, scholars, and laypersons discuss intense religious topics. Binkley's courses had always been robust and were usually taught by university faculty renowned in their fields. What could have been a run-of-the-mill Baptist Bible study morphed into a philosophical conversation on the origins of scripture, issues with inerrancy, and how to read the Bible without offering condemnation.

93

SAFFRON CROSS

It hadn't occurred to me before the invitation to teach, but Binkley's classes were the perfect place to encourage my devout Hindu monk into the Christian balance of our sabbath-keeping. Binkley's classes were like Sunday school on steroids—and looked more like Swami's hearty *Bhagavad Gita* lectures than anything Fred would have experienced when we attended a Baptist church during middle school.

Fred and I recommitted to the thirty-minute drive. I prepared one lecture on Hinduism, and he prepared another. I discovered how much Eastern richness I'd soaked up in just a few short years. Fred's nagging and drilling about this Hindu ritual or that Swami sermon had actually formed me more than I realized, and I had acquired a beginner's knowledge of Gaudiya Vaishnavism.

✝ ॐ ✝ ॐ ✝ ॐ ✝ ॐ ✝ ॐ ✝ ॐ ✝ ॐ ✝ ॐ ✝ ॐ ✝ ॐ ✝ ॐ ✝

Fred and I kept a small potted garden on the front and back concrete slabs of our one-bedroom apartment. We learned quickly that these spaces only received a half-day of sun, which translated into a growing season best suited for herbs and smaller flowers. Vegetables seeded in this kind of circumstance resulted in disappointment.

During the second year of our marriage, Fred and I planted orange and yellow marigold seeds. Marigolds are a staple in Hindu worship; they are the hearty flowers that adorn altars in the form of garlands and rest at the lotus feet of deities.

That year, our marigolds bloomed three days before Pentecost in an auspicious explosion of blood-orange buds that resembled tongues of fire. We agreed that these luscious first fruits should be offered to God in a small, interfaith ceremony at our home altar. Fred plucked the tiny bundles from their soil and prepared them for Hindu *puja* (worship). Hindus offer flowers, food, water, and whatever they have to God—an act of devotion, reverence, and dependence for our basic needs. Offering is also a way to integrate our material lives with our spiritual paths.

Fred gathered his supplies: a silver tray, a stick of incense, the *ghee* lamp, and a brass bell, used to drown out any mundane sounds during worship. We sat on the carpet before our altar, bowed in obeisance to the icon of Christ, photos of Gaura-Nitai deities, and a portrait of Swami. We played quiet chanting of the Holy Name, lit the incense and *ghee* lamp, and began our service.

Fred was meticulous in his liturgical moves, like the most orthodox of Christian priests. He held our baby marigold, fresh from its home, between his forefinger and thumb, circling the photos of the deities, his *guru*, and Christ. In his left hand, he rang the brass bell. He offered each framed photo the sweet smell of incense, circling with his right hand and filling our tiny living room with the scent of lavender. He chanted mantras, the sacred lines he learned as a priest. When he finished, he placed the flower before the icon of Christ.

Fred read scripture from the ninth chapter of the *Bhagavad Gita*, verses that denote instructions for offering God what you have. I read the Twenty-third Psalm and wept.

It was nothing new for me to cry during worship or before an altar. On many occasions, I'd been so overcome with emotion when I approached God that I couldn't hold back tears. Fred touched my knee, and I flubbed through David's psalm. The warmth of his hand made me remember that this is what I had always wanted—someone with whom to share my faith.

As my mind turned to gratitude, I prayed, *Thank you, God, for sending me what I've always needed through this extraordinary partner whose religion looks and feels different from mine, which makes sharing it all the more beautiful. Amen.*

I was no longer alone in my faith walk; I was walking a path with Fred. And here we were, having muddled through sabbath-keeping routines, discovering how to worship the God who had been revealed to us through Christ, deities, and Swami. This was all happening on the brink of the magical season called Pentecost in which languages and differences are set aside, and we truly begin to *understand* one another.

If Fred and I had decided to worship separately, we wouldn't have had these moments. We wouldn't have blended these richly devotional traditions and found harmony. But this moment hadn't come without struggle; it resulted from making mistakes, blaming each other, and finally uniting. If we hadn't made our golden rule of always worshiping together, we would have missed an evening like this one, where the two ancient traditions intertwined at a makeshift home-altar in North Carolina three days before Pentecost.

CHAPTER

VEGETARIANISM

If anyone offers me with devotion and purity a leaf, a flower, fruit or water,
I will accept that offering of devotion. Whatever you do, whatever you eat,
whatever you offer or give away, whatever austerities you perform . . .
do that as an offering unto me.

Bhagavad Gita: Its Feeling and Philosophy, 9.26–27

Fred and I continued to muddle our way through Christian-Hindu Sundays to find those electric Pentecost moments. When we experienced one, we patted each other on the back, proud of ourselves for living out a success-ful interfaith marriage—at least on Sundays. But there were six other days of interfaith living to contend with, and Hindus don't relegate their faiths to tidy boundaries. There is no sense of where one's spiritual path ends and secular life begins.

For devout Hindus, devotion is a 24-7 posture toward God. The deep faith they aspire to cannot be sustained by a weekly sixty-minute church obligation. God is not narrowly packed into the Hindu's schedule; rather,

God is the hub of a wheel, the center by which no hours are left untouched with spiritual richness.

Hindus' God-centric lifestyle is reflected in their culture. Our Indian honeymoon left me dazzled with the blurry edges of the Gaudiya Vaishnava faith that kept temple rhythms integrated into daily life. Most importantly, Hindus have taken an unavoidable human act—eating—and amalgamated it with devotion toward God.

Hindus call food *prasad,* or translated literally, *grace. Prasad* is not a value meal, an expensive steak dinner, or a snack to tide us over. *Prasad* is sacred, spiritual sustenance—and its preparation is a primary spiritual practice of devout Hindus.

Prasad is like consecrated Christian Communion—the holy food that feeds us with gifts of restoration, community, and remembrance. Ideally, this spiritual food is homegrown, harvested, prepared, offered to God, and eaten for every meal.

† ॐ † ॐ † ॐ † ॐ † ॐ † ॐ † ॐ † ॐ † ॐ † ॐ † ॐ †

My lesson on Hindu *prasad* unfolded slowly, as Fred hadn't disclosed his near decade-worth of vegetarian living before our first date. But like all good girls reared in the South to be polite company, I was poised to take cues from his meal selection.

"What are you getting?" I asked him on our first date.

"I am a vegetarian, so I'm going to have the vegetable quesadillas. But you can order whatever you'd like; it won't bother me."

This was the first and only lie Fred ever told me. I knew it was a lie because after I became a committed vegetarian, I discovered that a front row seat to someone else eating meat can be very disturbing.

"So, you don't eat meat?"

"Nope."

"Do you eat fish?"

"No."

"Eggs?"

"No."

Fred ticked off the Gaudiya Vaishnava laundry list of dietary restrictions: no eggs, alcohol, fish, gelatin, or marshmallows; onions, garlic, and mushrooms were also to be avoided.

I swallowed the lump of sympathy hanging in my throat. How could anyone live without marshmallows and Jell-O?

But the secret to Fred's religious diet was the amazing food he did eat—food that, as my relatives would say, "Makes you wanna slap yo Mama!" On subsequent dates, Fred took me on a culinary safari—a tour of the richest, spiciest, most delicious international food I'd ever encountered. Over time, I hardly noticed the absence of a carnivorous entrée—or marshmallows.

When Fred wasn't around, I regressed into my old habits and stuck with the standbys of meat and potatoes. This sputtering system of dietary segregation worked decently, until one day the staunch Hindu vegetarian asked me to marry him. I was faced with a daunting but necessary—even inspiring—decision: vegetarianism would have to be one of the compromises of our Christian-Hindu partnership.

But old habits die hard and almost always require help from Jesus. The season of Lent seemed like a good time to get started.

✝ ॐ ✝ ॐ ✝ ॐ ✝ ॐ ✝ ॐ ✝ ॐ ✝ ॐ ✝ ॐ ✝ ॐ ✝ ॐ ✝ ॐ ✝ ॐ ✝

"This is my *last* sausage patty, I promise."

Fred and my mother rolled their eyes as I nearly inhaled the crispy, fried goodness.

"Um . . . uh, maybe just *one* more," I mumbled, mouth full.

I walked from Binkley's fellowship hall to its kitchen, where disapproving youth group kids slapped serving number three of my Shrove Tuesday meal onto a plate.

Before seminary, marking the season of Lent by giving up a food or some activity for forty days was a foreign concept to this Southern Baptist. At divinity school, I learned to join my Methodist colleagues on their Lenten journeys but with far less piety and intention. I normally made a spur of the moment decision to give up a week of chocolate or sitcoms. But now, as the fiancée to a former Hindu monk, I was embarking on the season with some semblance of a plan to ensure the nutritional survival of my forthcoming marriage. I ate my fill of pancakes and sausage patties, and then I became a vegetarian.

✝ ॐ ✝ ॐ ✝ ॐ ✝ ॐ ✝ ॐ ✝ ॐ ✝ ॐ ✝ ॐ ✝ ॐ ✝ ॐ ✝ ॐ ✝

Ash Wednesday began with a terrible stomachache and a vigor to avoid meat. Had I written out my Lenten covenant, it would have looked something like this:

"Dear Lord, my stomach hurts, which will probably make it easier not to eat meat for forty days. But, in case I feel better tomorrow, guide me through this vegetarian wilderness that will help me in my marriage to a devout Gaudiya Vaishnava. Should I live until Easter, I promise I will limit meat to very small cheats when Fred is not around. Help me, Jesus. I know you distributed fish at the feeding of the five thousand, but I'm sure it could have been black bean burgers had there been more time and preparation. Thank you. Amen."

I marched through Lent with a practical focus and a keen sense of the time limit. But forty days of successful vegetarianism had the spiritual side effects of a clearer heart and head. Week by week, God softened my carnivorous rigidity with love and hope. I had answered both the church's invitation to mark sacred time and Fred's invitation to build an interfaith marriage. Easter arrived not with "Alleluia, it's over!" but, "Alleluia, there may be something to this meat-free living."

What began as a means of survival flowed into a desire to learn more about the spiritual benefits of a lifestyle that Hindu scripture revealed centuries ago. Vegetarianism would not only be beneficial to my marriage but would also affect my Christian walk.

I kept a meat-free diet after Easter, but ate fish, eggs, and gelatin, because, at that time, life seemed impossible without fried shrimp, omelets, and lime Jell-O. Luckily, my carnivorous hankerings stayed at bay until my wedding day when I can only determine that one of two things must have happened.

First, I hadn't planned well. Dietary restrictions were the last thing on my mind during the marathon that is a wedding weekend. Second, perhaps

I had, in some subconscious way, determined that this would be my *last* chance to eat beef. Psychologists everywhere would likely agree that reason number two fueled excuse number one.

In the frantic hours before "I do," my bridesmaids and I made a pit stop at the nearest fast food joint.

"What do you want to eat, Dana? You *have* to eat something!"

And because garden veggie patties and sesame tofu are not on the menu at Burger King, I said fiddle-de-dee to my newfound vegetarianism and gobbled up a cheeseburger, itchy with guilt. And I didn't confess this misstep to Fred until after the marriage license was signed, witnessed, and mailed. He forgave me.

But the siren calls of cheeseburgers continued. My father-in-law became a perpetrator in the game when he played "Cheeseburger in Paradise" on repeat during long boat rides. Then, just before lakeside dinners, he'd whisper to me: "You want me to sneak a *real* burger on the grill for you when Freddy isn't looking, Dana?"

I reluctantly replied, "No thanks," but only because Fred was around. I wanted to take my vegetarian commitment seriously—even if I was struggling.

†☃†☃†☃†☃†☃†☃†☃†☃†☃†☃†☃†☃†

At the two-year mark of my vegetarianism, I'd survived Lent and Jimmy Buffet. But when I drove by fast food establishments and saw patrons holding golden buns in yellow wrappers, I felt just the tiniest bit hostile. I asked Fred what to do.

"Pray that God will take away your desire for a cheeseburger."

"What?" I balked, like he was speaking another language.

"Ask God for help. Remember, you asked Jesus to help you through Lent. Ask God to help you *not* crave a cheeseburger now."

Fred was never one to petition the Divine for assistance with mundane human requests, especially those he deemed "first world problems." Cheeseburgers fell into that category, and if I prayed for anything remotely ridiculous aloud, he'd retort, "Dana, God has a life. Your prayer for Rack

Room to carry size five dress shoes is not a priority." So, I pushed for clarification on his suggestion of a cheeseburger prayer intervention.

"You're telling me that I should *ask* God to help me not want a cheeseburger?"

"Yes." Fred knew where I was going. "You're not asking God for something material, Dana. You're asking God to *help* you with the spiritual practice of not consuming meat."

Spiritual practice. I had forgotten. Giving up meat for Lent had softened my heart toward vegetarianism; but since then, I had only fixated on the grief of living with a man who would never treat me to a filet mignon on Valentine's Day.

Lent had been an easier season for vegetarianism because Christians around the world were in it together. Whether they had given up TV or sweets, added a daily meditation or scripture reading, there had been accountability and support among the body of Christ. You *knew* other Christians were moving through the wilderness with you. Now, I was a lone Protestant trying to kick a beef habit for the sake of her marriage to a man who had squelched his dietary demons ten years ago. I had begun the vegetarian journey with God, but I had left God behind after Easter.

Through Fred's support, I learned that I could pray for God to help me conquer my cheeseburger cravings, and I would not be the equivalent of an evangelical dieter. I simply wanted to share an important spiritual practice I did not yet understand with a man I loved more than anything else.

✝ ॐ ✝ ॐ ✝ ॐ ✝ ॐ ✝ ॐ ✝ ॐ ✝ ॐ ✝ ॐ ✝ ॐ ✝ ॐ ✝ ॐ ✝

God answered my cheeseburger prayer when Fred and I celebrated our second wedding anniversary at Audarya monastery in northern California, where Fred had spent one-and-a-half years of his cloistered tenure.

I'd never experienced a monastic setting. Pious Duke Divinity School friends had sacrificed fall and spring breaks to work alongside Trappist monks and keep sanctified church hours. But that had never been my bag.

Before we boarded the plane, Fred prepared me for the intensity of observing the monastic schedule he'd known for nearly five years: early morning and evening worship, morning and afternoon service, scripture classes, as well as *prasad* preparation and taking.

Audarya's rhythm was not that difficult to fall into because all its residents were fully involved in temple activities. It felt like the Hindu equivalent of Lent's accountability.

Fred and I became acquainted with two members of the community, a married European couple named Sanatana and Namaruci, who'd traveled to Audarya to offer three months of service. Their skills and kind hearts landed them in the temple kitchen where they prepared and offered the deities' three daily meals. The remnants of those offerings became *prasad* for the monastic community and guests.

Fred had tried to explain the spiritual significance of vegetarianism to me when we were first married, but the same idealism that surfaced during the Swami months flung our lessons into arguments. His impatience with my continued burger cravings led to my accusatory statements of his elitism. I needed to learn the importance of *prasad* from someone who wasn't already frustrated with my meat-craving tendencies.

I watched Sanatana's and Namaruci's meticulous food preparations, offerings, and service, all completed to the soundtrack of the Lord's Holy Name. Eventually, I worked up the courage to ask Sanatana to teach me about Hindu vegetarian spirituality, and he obliged.

We spent the afternoon hours between the lunch and dinner meals seated on thin green cushions on the *prasad* room floor. I asked questions, and he offered thoughtful responses in his British accent. Perhaps it was his patience, accent, the temple atmosphere, or the ten days of spiritual food I'd already consumed, but I finally understood the Hindu spirituality of vegetarianism.

Sanatana was an encyclopedia of Gaudiya Vaishnava dietary practices. He knew everything—why vegetarianism is spiritually essential, which foods are acceptable, why they are offered, and how they become *prasad*. I listened like an eager graduate student at the feet of an established professor, feverishly taking notes. For the first time in two years, I appreciated the requisite dietary compromise of my Christian-Hindu interfaith marriage.

Sanatana explained that food undergoes a spiritual journey to *prasad*; the process is an act of devotion, praise, and thanksgiving toward God. It is worship through meal preparation, a way of connecting with the Divine through something we do each day. The food at Audarya is grown and harvested with this intention. Trained *pujaris* like Sanatana and Fred offer the food with mantras and devoted hearts; God's acceptance makes it consecrated *prasad*. Nonmonastic Christians would likely grow weary of this practice because it would mean having three meals at church or hiring a stay-at-home priest. A small derivative of this system is saying grace before meals, which has been adequate for American Protestants for centuries.

Devout Hindus believe the wisdom your family doctor offers at annual physicals: you are what you eat. But the Hindu imperative has less to do with heart disease and high blood pressure and more to do with awareness and experience.

The *Bhagavad Gita* categorizes food into three modes: goodness (*satva*), ignorance (*tamas*), and passion (*rajas*). The classification is based on how the food affects the person's mind once it is consumed.

Foods from the goodness category promote peace, well-being, health, clarity, and knowledge. They bring satisfaction to the body and mind. These foods coincide with modern nutritional guidelines: fruits, vegetables, grains, legumes, and dairy products. The one exception is sugar, which, in moderation, Gaudiya Vaishnavas consider to be in the mode of goodness. The devotee's spiritual goal is to eat mostly from the goodness category and eliminate ignorant and passionate foods.

Milk is the mother of all foods for Gaudiya Vaishnavas. It nourishes the brain so that the Hindu devotee can conceive deep philosophical concepts. This was contrary to my concept of milk, which I thought was to promote sleep. Milk and its by-products are essential to the Hindu diet because they come from the cow, which Gaudiya Vaishnavas consider to be the most sacred animal in the Vedic tradition. Cows are central to communal life; they are all-giving and generous because their milk provides a plethora of products for the monastery. Milk, curd, yogurt, cheese, and butter become food for offering, and *ghee* fuels *puja* (worship) lamps.

But the not-so-rosy side of Hindu dietary laws is what happens when we consume foods from the modes of ignorance and passion. Animal flesh, decomposing food, and fermented foods (alcohol) are all in the mode of ignorance because they dull the senses. According to devout Hindus, when we consume food from this category, it is difficult to appreciate and comprehend spiritual subject matters.

Passionate foods are those that are too extreme, spicy, salty, acidic, or oily. These foods excite the senses and leave the body craving more. Hindus also consider garlic and onion to be passionate foods because they have strong flavors and odors that overstimulate the senses.

The Hindu food guidelines for goodness, ignorance, and passion all stem from the philosophy that the human body is a vehicle for service. Therefore it needs to operate at a highly efficient level that minimizes any impediments to heightened spiritual awareness.

Eating foods from the mode of goodness was all I had been doing for ten days at Audarya because Sanatana and Namaruci had chosen the foods for me. The temple diet, coupled with the peace of the northern California Redwoods, had given me more spiritual clarity to understand the food groupings Sanatana explained. But I still couldn't grasp the seemingly Old Testament concept of offering food to God.

The importance of offering food was amplified in the monastic setting where all activities were God-centric. Three times per day, Sanatana and Namaruci slid open the wooden door to a sacristy-like room that held the deities' plates, cups, and worship equipment. I caught glimpses of the shelves, cupboards, and storage for God's accoutrements, but I never asked to go in. I didn't feel I had the piety required to enter a room so intimate and sacred.

Like preparations for a high mass, offering meals to God came with impeccable standards: a clean body, clean hands, clear mind, and food that had not yet been tasted or enjoyed prior to God's eating. A devotee with a servant's heart chanted mantras to the Gaura-Nitai deities and offered the meal. But I couldn't keep from wondering if it was necessary. Did God really need food?

When I asked Sanatana about this, he shifted on his green mat and answered, "We offer food because God has given us a wonderful opportunity to use one of the most fundamental necessities of life to awaken a process of love and devotion. If we can utilize this necessity of life to deepen our love for God, then it is of great use to our spiritual progress."

I was amazed that something as mundane as fixing lunch could turn into an act of worship. But it could—because God doesn't really want my grilled cheese sandwich. God wants my time, love, and devotion. Incorporating my attention into such a daily task could grow my relationship with God because it focuses the day on what's most important.

Hindu *prasad* rituals reminded me of the Christian Communion table. At this table, all are welcomed; all are loved; and ultimate grace is found in consecrated bread and wine. We've been taught to remember this miracle by God, incarnate as Jesus.

This system of turning mundane mealtimes into an act of worship was a rich practice in a monastery, but was it practical for the real world? Could you keep such high standards and consistent rhythms in a household where both partners work and have to meet the demands of noncloistered life?

Fred's spiritual idealism usually kept him from completing the *prasad* ritual at our home altar. He often chose not to offer food that hadn't been made from scratch or in the best of circumstances. This meant we usually skipped the Hindu ritual and offered a prayer of grace instead.

The day after my intensive lesson with Sanatana, Fred and I sat on the wooden floor of Swami's room in Audarya, and he encouraged us to think about offering food at home differently.

"Don't wait to offer food made from scratch; do it now."

The *guru* gave us a gentle reminder not to postpone spiritual practice because of spiritual idealism. After all, what God really wants is our devotion, not our dinner.

But was that jarred pasta sauce that contains onions and garlic *really* good enough to offer God?

"Yes," Swami said, emphatically.

"The deities are eating the *feeling* of your offering, not your food."

According to Hindu scripture, jarred spaghetti sauce or an intricate Indian meal cooked from scratch is not what God is looking for anyway. "If anyone offers me with devotion and purity a leaf, a flower, fruit or water, I will accept that offering of devotion. Whatever you do, whatever you eat, whatever you offer or give away, whatever austerities you perform . . . do that as an offering unto me."

Leaves, flowers, fruits, and water are four basic elements that are readily accessible in most communities and circumstances. These are not fancy meals, rare ingredients, or materials that are difficult to obtain. The simplicity with which Krishna asks his devotees to remember him indicates that the essential component of the act is devotion, not food.

I heard Swami explain that offering food connects our human ability to love with the biological need to sustain ourselves. When we grow, prepare, and offer food, we include God in that process, and we are mindful of the one who provided the sustenance and grace.

After food becomes grace through devotion, humans consume it and receive the blessedness of its consecration. But there are still standards for taking *prasad,* and I've made a fool of myself many times by forgetting the rules. Audarya was no exception.

For example, there is no smelling or tasting food before it's offered. Food is meant to be enjoyed by God *first*. I've embarrassed myself in Hindu settings by exclaiming, "Oh! That smells so good!" only to be met with an elbow in my rib and an evil eye from Fred.

Hindu kitchens are holy and sacred places. In temples like Audarya, all kitchen supplies, cooking utensils, pots, and pans are kept separate from the room that is used to take *prasad*. There's even a separate mop and broom for the Hindu kitchen, so that no contamination from the *prasad* room interferes with the holy practice of cooking for God.

Once food is prepared and offered, it is never served directly from the pots in which it was prepared or the spoons with which it was stirred. It is transferred to a separate container used only for serving, and it is dished out onto stainless steel plates by humble monks with clean hands and good hearts.

Just as Christians *take* Communion, *prasad* is *taken*, not eaten, in a room where practitioners sit on the floor and eat with their right hands. No utensils or napkins are used because, according to Ayurvedic principles, digestion begins with the fingers, which contain enzymes that help the process. My germophobe personality has a hard time with this.

Second helpings are only served by someone who has washed his or her hands and agrees to scoop another helping for everyone. Leftover *prasad* is kosher to take so long as it was offered at a previous mealtime and had not gone bad or sour. This rule was a drag if you're like me and crave snacks at inopportune and inappropriate times when there is no consecrated *prasad* available.

Thanks to my long days in Audarya and the lessons from Sanatana, Namaruci, Swami, and the other residents, I understood the gift that Fred had given me through our vegetarian compromise. I now looked at my food as a means to spiritual growth. Offering my food made me mindful of its source and my dependence upon God. And this is a God who wants my time and devotion. I experienced Communion—grace—every day, all day.

It took me two years of a waffling, fledgling Christian vegetarianism to discover this truth. And only then did I stop craving cheeseburgers.

CHAPTER

RELIGIOUS DIFFERENCES

Be always humble, gentle, and patient. Show your love by being tolerant with one another. Do your best to preserve the unity which the Spirit gives by means of the peace that binds you together.

Ephesians 4:2-3, GNT

Shortly after our second wedding anniversary, a friend asked Fred and me to be honest with him about the difficulties of interfaith marriage.

"Like, *really* honest," he said.

He must have sensed that I'm one for putting on a show of politeness, carefully hoisting the trouble-free marriage façade with quivering arms. But truthfully, the first two years of our matrimonial journey were strained with the stress of navigating materialism, sabbath-keeping, and vegetarianism. And those were only the practical activities of surviving a Christian-Hindu life.

What remained was the icy tension of philosophical differences that, in ripe conditions, bubbled to the surface with bursts of caustic anger and seething words. That's when things fell apart.

"You're awfully quiet, my sweet," Fred pried cautiously.

"Just thinking," I replied guardedly.

"About what?" he pushed further.

"Nothing."

"Dana—what is it?" he insisted.

"Nothing, Fred. It's nothing."

"You can tell me."

"No, I can't tell you. Because you'll get angry and defensive and then we cannot have a conversation."

"I don't do that."

"Ummm—yes, you do!"

"Tell me—what are you thinking about?" he tried again. "I know you're only quiet when something is on your mind."

"I'm just frustrated," I finally admitted.

"Why?"

"Because of what you said last night before bed—that you don't think my Christianity is as deep as your Hinduism."

"I never said that."

"Well, maybe you didn't say that, but you implied it."

"How did I imply it?"

"When you kept pushing me on theological questions I couldn't answer."

"You were being vague," Fred defended.

"And you're a spiritual elitist!" I snapped back.

The initial patience Fred showed early in our courtship seemed to have withered away, or at least worn thin—and mine was doing the same. Although I wanted a marriage without disagreements, I understood logically that partners disagree, get angry, and feel like things are spinning out of control. Even two Christians passionately devoted to the same Jesus have these moments. The likelihood of not seeing eye-to-eye was even higher in the marriage of a Baptist minister and a former Hindu monk.

Fred and I were operating from two inherently different frameworks. Our personal convictions about spiritual depth, spiritual authority, and deity worship fed fiery disagreements that couldn't be appeased with an extra ritual or dietary changes. The peace I'd felt during our Indian honeymoon—the excitement of two pilgrims on an adventure to solidify an east-meets-west partnership—was crushed under the weight of sustaining our interfaith life.

Fred's spiritual idealism coupled with my fears, feelings of inadequacy, and longing for control tumbled us into a space so seemingly irreconcilable that I was certain a harmonious Christian-Hindu marriage was not attainable. The two religions felt too different, and we cared too much. This is when my stomach dropped, I cried rivers of tears, and I worried that this interfaith marriage was over.

†ॐ†ॐ†ॐ†ॐ†ॐ†ॐ†ॐ†ॐ†ॐ†ॐ†ॐ†

My feelings of spiritual inadequacy hadn't begun in our interfaith relationship. They were birthed in the Duke Divinity School classrooms in which I was surrounded by brilliant students who could articulate complex doctrines as easily as they rattled off grocery lists. My inability to keep up with them planted seeds of insecurity that grew into destructive weeds of self-depreciation.

Fred's circle of Gaudiya Vaishnava friends were like the Duke students I'd known. They dove intentionally into the Vedic canon and commentaries and inhaled the sacred teachings. Swami encouraged thoughtful application of scripture. He posed that a questioning, hungry faith is a healthy faith, and that scripture study is balanced well with heartfelt devotion for worship and service. Fred's monastic tenure at Audarya was his equivalent of a Master of Divinity degree—only it seemed as if he had graduated with honors, while I had barely passed.

I had not adopted a theologian's well-reasoned faith. I could boil my spirituality down to two scripture essentials: "'Love one another'" (John 13:34) and "'Just as you did it to one of the least of these . . . you did it to me'" (Matt. 25:40). These verses produced my bumper sticker theology: *Love Jesus? Love people.*

Gaudiya Vaishnavism has similar devotional ideals but also a strong focus on making personal spiritual advancement, encouraging Hindus' self-reflective habits of concentrated meditation, scripture study, and the rituals that center them on the Divine.

111

Since I'd married Fred, I felt I'd won front-row seats to this super concentrated God-centric faith, yet the intensity of Hindu spirituality made me panic. Instead of using the opportunity to cultivate my own spiritual depth, I spiraled into self-doubt. Though I initially returned to a deeper pursuit of Christ and spirituality when we first began dating, I hadn't consistently given into that thirst the way Fred wanted me to—and he told me so.

Fred's words made me resentful. I ticked off the list of the saintly things I'd done since our eHarmony days: becoming a vegetarian, going on a sex-free honeymoon in India, establishing our sabbath-keeping routine, and attending hours of Swami's sermons and Hindu worship services. I felt I'd grown exponentially, and I begrudged Fred for not offering me ceaseless accolades. But those shiny accomplishments were only on the Hindu side of our life, and I'd neglected the steady cultivation of the Christian aspect of myself. This made my heart shrink with the regret of imbalance and lost time, and the only thing I could do was to soothe myself with quiet mantras of hymns like "Oh, How I Love Jesus" and "Just as I Am." I was instantly transported back to the comfort of my simple and familiar Baptist roots.

✝ ॐ ✝ ॐ ✝ ॐ ✝ ॐ ✝ ॐ ✝ ॐ ✝ ॐ ✝ ॐ ✝ ॐ ✝ ॐ ✝ ॐ ✝

Fred is unabashedly committed to his *guru*, God, and his Hindu faith. He devoutly approaches the Divine and asks, "How can I serve God today?"

From that humble viewpoint, it's easy to understand Fred's frustration with what he perceived to be Christianity's group prayer for material comfort and prosperity. But I took this personally.

"All Christians do is ask God for things." Fred declared as we drove home from church.

"That's not true!" I rebutted.

"Yes, it is! You think God is your personal vending machine."

Fred's disappointment in Christianity stemmed from his middle school observations of practitioners who lacked philosophical brawn but had plenty of hypocrisy sprinkled with a penchant of, what Anne Lamott calls, God as "cosmic bellhop."

Just as I began to open my mouth and defend my religion from its reputation of praying for shoe sales and parking spaces, the brief silence was interrupted with a Christian radio broadcast of a listener thanking Jesus for a luxury automobile.

"That's not unique to American Protestantism!" I pointed to the radio and snapped the power button off. "Persons in all religions ask God to fulfill their individual desires."

"True," Fred softened, sensing my hurt feelings. "And people have to start somewhere. But eventually we should all move beyond reliance on God to make our temporary lives comfortable. God has desires that represent an opportunity to serve."

"That is such a Hindu thing to say!" I responded.

The sense that God had a life was a Hindu bridge that was difficult to cross into Christianity. Vedic scripture offered long, detailed descriptions of God's holy pastimes, personality, and relationships, which, Fred argued, made it much easier to be close to and to love God.

"How can you be close to someone you don't really know?" he questioned me.

"We know tons about Jesus!"

"Really? What was he doing from ages twelve to thirty?"

"Uh. I don't know. Hanging out in India?"

Fred forced a quiet laugh, and we both felt temporary relief.

But Fred's largest frustration with Christianity is that Christians don't model what they do know about Jesus Christ—and that there is a great discrepancy between who people think Jesus is and who he really was. And Fred loves the *real* Jesus; he just can't figure out why many Christians don't act like him.

Still, Fred admits that there are Christians who are Christlike, and he wants me to get to know them. So, instead of jewelry, cashmere, perfume, flowers, or chocolate for Christmas and birthdays, Fred gives me books on Christian saints, mystics, and church leaders whom he thinks embodied Jesus. This is *so* romantic and not at all annoying. Once I let go of my bitterness, I end up appreciating his gesture of finding me guides who exemplify the Christian spiritual ideal—because that is what Fred has come to know through Swami.

†ॐ†ॐ†ॐ†ॐ†ॐ†ॐ†ॐ†ॐ†ॐ†ॐ†ॐ†ॐ†

Gurus are the essential source of spiritual authority on the Hindu's path. Gaudiya Vaishnava gurus are part of a long line of disciplic succession (*paramapara*) described in scripture. *Gurus* are Hindus' miniature version of God, here by grace to show us how to love and serve.

Each *guru* cultivates *bhakti* (love) for Krishna by adopting the spiritual practices given to him or her by a *guru*. Fred's *guru*, Swami Bhakti Vedanta Tripurari Maharaja, offers his students what his *gurus*, Srila A. C. Bhaktivedanta Swami Prabhupada and Srila B. R. Sridhar Maharaja, offered him: insight and example on the spiritual path. Swami has been a monk for four decades, during which he's practiced, served, written, and taught others how to serve God. His position as an advanced spiritual soul is evidenced by the respect he is offered. When he enters a room, visitors and students touch their heads to the ground in reverence. His presence is mystical; people want to be dear to him because they know he is dear to God.

This reverence for a *guru* would alarm some Christians—certainly Southern Baptists who tend to be defensive when another human being tells them how to behave spiritually. Baptist ecclesiology, after all, includes an anti-catholic recipe of autonomy with a dash of nonconformity. Swami's position as a *guru* is a far cry from the Baptist notion that faith is direct line between God and the individual. Third-party involvement goes against our embrace of the doctrine of universal priesthood, or the common phrase written on Baptist worship bulletins, "Every member a minister." The *guru's* status and position within the mission is difficult for a Baptist to absorb because "Ain't nobody gonna tell me what to do but Jesus!"

Naturally, I was uncomfortable with the esteem in which Fred held Swami and with the authority and influence that Swami possessed. It wasn't that I was completely unfamiliar with the idea of a shepherd—I'd encountered many Baptist pastors who were respected and who held an elevated position of authority within the walls of a church—but not in the same way a *guru* does. Gaudiya Vaishnavas describe *gurus* as the active agent of Divinity, while scripture is the passive agent of Divinity.

Even though Swami wasn't my *guru*, my heart sped up whenever I encountered him, and I was as self-conscious as a teen with acne. I imagine it's the same feeling I'd have if Billy Graham or the pope knocked on our apartment door for afternoon tea. It's like a wind of divinity in the space where you're sitting, a miniature extension of God shrunken down to fit in the world.

But Fred's obedience and attention to such a spiritual third party was an early source of contention in our marriage. This was no fault of Swami's, or necessarily Fred's, but my Baptist and personal baggage made it difficult for me to accept the spiritual authority of another man besides Jesus.

Early on, I grabbed hold of free-floating anxiety that Fred would return to the monastery and to Swami. I was afraid that if he ever had to choose between the two of us, he'd choose his *guru* because it would be like choosing God. And that would be so much more peaceful than rehashing theological differences with a Christian wife.

Swami's visits and Fred's persistent pushing for greater spiritual depth made me certain I'd find a "Dear John" letter sitting on our altar one day. This uneasy feeling usually led to a release of unwarranted anger faster than churchgoers rushing to Sunday lunch. I was just the tiniest bit cantankerous about the whole thing.

My Clinical Pastoral Education supervisor once told me that anger almost always comes from a place of pain. I felt pain in what I perceived as Swami occupying a role that should now only be reserved for me. I felt Swami had Fred's ear, his attention, and his heart and that Fred had exchanged a cloistered life for a marriage of tension.

But my circumstantial evidence for such claims would not have held up in any court. Swami had no dark ulterior motives to steal Fred from me. And Fred had no desires to return to a life he felt he wasn't called to. But I had convinced myself that Fred was still heavy-laden with the burdens of regret, failure, relief, and missing the teacher whom he loved so dearly.

Aside from the principle of *guru*, I also wasn't keen on the notion of deity worship. I didn't know much about it, but I knew enough that it evoked my Old Testament-based fear of idolatry. Yet my anxiety and judgment melted under the warm *ghee* lamps, fragrant incense, and beauty of the Hindu scripture's description of God's form set in stone. I felt the same divinity I'd known when I placed sacred Communion elements in my mouth.

But I had one lingering suspicion: why were Hindus worshiping a deity when they could be out among the people, feeding the poor, helping the sick, visiting the imprisoned? My religion implored that this is where you find God—in people—not in a twelve-inch marble statue adorned with flowers and jewels. Lingering frustration remained the more I attended Hindu worship services, and I wrestled with the fact that Hindus poured time, money, and food into deity worship when there were plenty of God's children who needed care.

When I told Fred this, we again smacked right into the wall that is the intrinsic philosophical difference between Eastern and Western religion: the material life and the journey of the soul.

"Jesus teaches that he is present in the least of us; the hungry, poor, disadvantaged, and imprisoned. Taking care of these people is our service to God," I explained.

"I agree. Helping others is good for both the giver and receiver. But this temporary body is going to die no matter how much food we give it or how much medicine we take. It is the soul that needs nourishment."

"But how exactly are you nourishing the soul by clothing the deity and giving it food every day? Couldn't you mix it up a little? Feed the deity one day, feed the homeless the next?" I countered.

"You're missing the point. Giving our time and money to worship the deity and to support the temple where the deity resides means giving up material things that are only temporarily important to us. As we give these things to God we slowly realize that we are an eternal soul that is nourished by affectionately serving God. Otherwise, we think we are this temporary body that must take things from others to sustain a life that will ultimately end. And we won't see others as souls until we see ourselves in the same way. We can give them food, but how can we truly nourish them if we don't recognize their spiritual needs? It's like rescuing the coat of a drowning man and claiming you saved him. By only preserving the body, we neglect the soul."

"But Christians share Jesus' love by loving others. We share love because God has loved us," I said.

"You sound like a Hindu," Fred replied.

CHAPTER

AUDARYA

Above all, clothe yourselves with love,
which binds everything together in perfect harmony.

Colossians 3:14, NRSV

When we honeymooned in the holiest city I'd ever known, I felt sure that our interfaith partnership would survive. India's spirituality whispered to me that there were many adventures to be had and much room to grow; marrying a former Hindu monk would be the best thing I could do for my Christianity.

But then Fred and I spent the next year and a half organizing our complex religious lives, ironing out the practicalities of an east-meets-west marriage. In two years, we'd learned more about each other and our religions through endless theological conversations and a dozen heated arguments. Yet after all these battles, we found ourselves at an impasse, stuck in the sludge of resentment and frustration. Was our marriage breaking under the weight of two religions at opposite ends of the spectrum? Could we reconcile Hinduism's intense spiritual practice with Christianity's simple love of Jesus? Seeing eye to eye was becoming rare, and it seemed that even the loveliest of hybrid blooms had thorns.

I didn't know it at the time but in this troubled season, Fred had no second thoughts about our union. He remained steady, continuing his efforts to strengthen our interfaith path and my Christianity—all while deepening his Hinduism. But even he sensed the need for another unifying spiritual respite like the one we'd experienced in India. He longed to show me a sacred place where his faith could unfold before me, just as it had seven thousand miles from home in an ashram with no toilet paper. He yearned for a space that would offer me universal explanations, consolations, connections, and reassurances of our vows to grow together in faith and love. To accomplish this, we booked flights for the trek to Audarya, the Hindu monastery where he spent the most formational year and a half of his life.

Fred and I journeyed to northern California in the midst of one of our most hurtful disagreements. Personal religious convictions that couldn't or wouldn't budge hung heavily over us, tied tight with invisible threads of deep-seated opinions and personal faith histories. But Fred was committed to wrestling our way through our challenges, and we were going to do it within the confines of temple walls.

Fred and I boarded a plane from Raleigh to San Francisco sixteen days before our second wedding anniversary, when my fear of "Dear John" letters and interfaith nitpicking were at an all-time high. The voyage to India had been the foundation of our relationship; Audarya would be the keystone.

I hauled my bitterness onto the Boeing 737 like a child's frayed carry-on, bursting at the seams with *guru* paranoia, acrimony over my lack of spiritual depth, and confusion over deity worship and Hinduism's internal focus.

The scrunched airplane seat reminded me that our India pilgrimage had felt less constrictive and threatening. Swami didn't live in India; Fred hadn't served a monastery there; and the country's chaos meant that he wouldn't have likely chosen to remain in the land of near misses. But Audarya packed its own punch; it was the place where Fred said his *guru* planted seeds deep within his heart. I wondered if Fred would swap his wedding ring for a saffron robe at the first sight of the temple. After all, it was what I deemed the easier, preferred spiritual path.

I gripped my insecurities as tightly as I clenched the armrests. I loved Fred so much, and I wondered if it would be unfair to drag him back to the challenges of interfaith living if he actually preferred a peaceful Hindu life.

My crazy-making had to stop—at least temporarily—because it was unwarranted, and I didn't want my negativity to color an opportunity to spend ten days focused on God. One of the most important tenets of inter-faith marriage I had learned was that communication—even awkward, blubbering, or incoherent communication—was essential.

"Fred, I need to tell you something."

Fred leaned in close and squeezed my hands as I prattled on about my Audarya fears. His intense listening instantly calmed my anxiety, and when I finished, he offered me tender assurances about our marriage and all the reasons he'd chosen our path. Somewhere over the continental United States, with swollen eyes and drenched tissues, I suspected that our Christian-Hindu marriage may just have some roots and that Fred would likely join me on the plane ride home. But my old foe, fear, would creep up again, and Audarya would be a ten-day spiritual lesson of push-and-pull.

† ॐ † ॐ † ॐ † ॐ † ॐ † ॐ † ॐ † ॐ † ॐ † ॐ † ॐ † ॐ †

Audarya is a twenty-acre monastery tucked into a remote Redwood ridge of northern California. Nearly thirty minutes from the nearest valley boasting luscious vineyards and wine tasting tours, the monastic com-plex is situated on Panorama Way, a winding path indicative of the view to come: lush, green trees touching blue skies in all directions.

This cloistered community is home to a handful of monks, a dozen cows, one barn cat and her canine colleague, a peacock, and a *guru*. They share life, meals, and religion on this off-the-grid beacon of devotional solitude. Terraced vegetable and flower gardens, a temple, a kitchen, cow barns, cabins, a bathhouse, and yurts comprise the grounds. Solar pan-els, a well, and a small crew of hard-working community members keep the place running with an unabashed commitment to serving God and their *guru*.

The temple is Audarya's spiritual focal point. Located on the edge of the ridge, this holy center was hand-constructed by the monks and Swami.

The temple's interior walls are Japanese plaster painted in earth tones to match the bamboo floors and modern Asian design. Symmetrical windows and glass doors dot the length of each wall, giving God and worshiper breathtaking views of the hillside. During our summer stay, the glass doors were opened, allowing the peaceful worship space to fill with a breeze from the nearby Pacific Ocean.

Sri Sri Gaura-Nityananda are Audarya's primary deities. Hindu deities are nearly always found in pairs, with one essence reflecting the other in perfect balance and harmony. Surrounded by fresh flowers from the garden, Gaura-Nityananda reside on an altar resembling a Jewish chuppah. Below the deities are photos of *gurus* in the Bhaktivinoda Parivara, the lineage of Gaudiya Vaishnavism from which Swami and his students hail. The altar is located in a small room called the sanctum sanctorum that sits separate from the main worship space. The sanctum sanctorum has sliding doors of frosted glass that open and close throughout the day according to a schedule.

A large wooden deck runs the back length of the temple building, and we would partake of lunchtime *prasad* here while mesmerized by the view. Across the gorge, trees blanket the adjacent hills and swallow memories of the outside world. The sun is a spotlight on creation, and only the moving shadows across the valley remind the spectator that time still exists.

† ॐ † ॐ † ॐ † ॐ † ॐ † ॐ † ॐ † ॐ † ॐ † ॐ † ॐ † ॐ †

Like our Indian honeymoon, Audarya's days began at 4:00 a.m. Fred showered while I life-coached myself from under the covers, just as I had in Vrindavan.

"Dana, get up. This will be good for you," I muttered to myself, prying the covers from my head.

"It'll be worth it," I thought I heard God reply.

It took nearly forty-five minutes to coax myself out of bed and into clothes, to wash my face and brush my teeth and hair amid northern California's chilliest hours.

Five minutes before worship was scheduled to begin, Fred pleaded, "Are you *finally* ready for *tilak*?"

I sighed. I had to get used to this life-revolving-around-God bit.

I slid over to him, frowning, and wondering why—once again—I'd agreed to *vacation* in a place whose docket began before dawn.

Fred dampened the palm of his right hand and swirled the yellow square made of clay collected from the banks of the Yamuna River. I watched him carefully as he gathered enough on the tip of his ring finger to make the long line from the center part of my hair to the middle of my nose. He stood back and assessed his work, grumbling something about me having my father's nose, the bridge of which is too thin, which makes applying *tilak* nearly impossible.

Fred shaped the clay into a neat, narrow V with a teardrop at the end, a symbol of Gaudiya Vaishnavism. I was an ordained Baptist minister wearing a visible sign of Hinduism—a colorful indication of my commitment to merge these two worlds.

Fred and I wrapped up tightly in wool *chaddars* and walked the short dirt path up the hill to the temple. The moon lit our way, and just like in India, I felt a burst of self-righteousness for being awake before the rest of the world.

The temple was warm inside, heated by soft lights and bundled-up devotees chanting *japa*. The door to the sanctum sanctorum was closed as everyone awaited morning *darshan*. Soft blue light crept through the ridge outside and a bell rang, signaling the beginning of *managala arati*, the most auspicious time of day to worship the Lord.

A conch shell sounded like a Jewish shofar and the doors slid open revealing the deities. Everyone dropped to their knees, chests pressed against the cool wooden floor and heads bowed in reverence to God. Dim temple lights reflected the soft, welcoming faces of the deities of Mahaprabhu and Nityananda, or Gaura-Nitai, the most magnanimous incarnations of God.

Morning worship included a one-hour liturgy of songs and prayers, a routine that all of the monks, including Fred, had memorized by heart. I clung to the printed lyrics of transliterated Sanskrit and sang with a groggy, off-pitch voice. A young *pujari* stood at the altar and offered incense, light, flowers, and fans to God on our behalf. He was the steady conductor of a carefully composed liturgy—a role that Fred had held during his time at the monastery.

On that first morning, Swami slipped in shortly before we began. He offered his own obeisance to the deities and then stood with us, like the gospel among the people. During worship, he played drums and harmonium and enthusiastically sang songs he'd known for four decades.

It was the first time I'd seen him in this role—worshiping God like the rest of us, albeit from a deeper perspective. As the sun rose in the California sky, Swami sang and prayed and danced, and I realized that he too was a pilgrim on the path.

After morning worship, some monks continued their prayers or read scripture while others began their day of *seva* (service)—milking cows, gardening, or preparing breakfast. Monks meticulously cooked and ritualistically offered three meals per day to the deities. The consecrated remnants of these offerings became *prasad* for the community members. The largest meal of the day was lunch, and afterward, everyone returned to his or her individual assignment.

My afternoon *seva* was nothing to sneeze at. I worked in the main building sweeping, dusting, and mopping the floors of the temple. In between duties, I'd stop and stare at the deities, soaking up the sanctity of the worship space. I was transported back to the silent Sunday afternoons of my youth when I wandered First Baptist Church's sanctuary looking for God in the brick crevices.

When Swami and the monks weren't engaged in their own *seva*, they spent hours discussing the complex philosophy of the religious tradition. Swami is a robust voice in Gaudiya Vaishnavism, which means there are books and articles to be written, edited, and published—and eager students waiting to devour them. Audarya's mood of service stood in close proximity with its dutiful obligation to study.

Everyone in Audarya called Fred by his initiated name, *Gauravani*, which is what I call him only when I want a sure-fire way to get his attention in a crowd of people. Although we were guests, Fred offered his service of IT support, web development, and errand running. But his favorite time was spent with the cows, lovingly scooping their excrement, feeding them alfalfa snacks, and scratching their necks.

At sunset, the monks finished their work and prepared their bodies, minds, and hearts for evening worship and scripture class. A light snack was served at 5:45 p.m., and the remains of the day signaled the casualness and ease of worn-out bodies. Golden light passed through the hillside, and it was time to close the day's God-focused routine.

After evening worship, we all sat cross-legged on the temple floor, settling down for an hour-long scripture study and discussion on inter-facing Gaudiya Vaishnava philosophy with modern culture and thought. On the evenings when there was no class, we watched Hindu-themed documentaries, which answered my age-old question, *What kind of movies do monks watch?*

The faithful *pujari* put the deities to rest at 8:00 p.m., and we all returned to our yurts or cabins for bed. With only one full day centered on God, my spirit had already been rocked into the peaceful lull of inten-tional community. I had a temporary amnesia for our interfaith marriage disagreements; I was happy to see Fred so content to serve his *guru* and spend time in community. More than that, he seemed content to share it with me.

✝ ॐ ✝ ॐ ✝ ॐ ✝ ॐ ✝ ॐ ✝ ॐ ✝ ॐ ✝ ॐ ✝ ॐ ✝ ॐ ✝ ॐ ✝

On that first night, once the California hillside was cloaked in pitch dark and everyone was asleep, an old anxiety crept up behind me. I tried to avoid it, the way you'd hide behind the aisles at the grocery store when you see an ex-boyfriend with his tall blond girlfriend, pushing a cart of your awkward memories.

But my uneasiness reminded me that I was still a restless sojourner with an imperfect interfaith marriage surrounded by people who were much closer to God than I was. I tried to push fear back, but it shouted in my ear that I was still a no-good pilgrim.

"Fred," I whispered.

"Yeah," he replied, half asleep, his back pressed against my arm.

"I'm a little scared."

He turned toward me, albeit reluctantly, out of husbandly obligation.

"Why are you scared? I'm right here," he mumbled.

"I'm not that kind of scared. I'm terrified that you and the monks here are so deep into your faiths—so close to God—and I don't know what I'm doing. I feel so far away from God."

He breathed deeply, and whispered, "Feeling far away from God is actually an indication of spiritual progress, Dana. The closer we are to God, the smaller we feel."

I hung onto his words.

"Now, go to sleep. We have to be back up at four," which was his polite way of ending the conversation.

I asked God to come a little closer and fell asleep.

✝ ॐ ✝ ॐ ✝ ॐ ✝ ॐ ✝ ॐ ✝ ॐ ✝ ॐ ✝ ॐ ✝ ॐ ✝ ॐ ✝ ॐ ✝ ॐ ✝

Despite Fred's encouraging words the night before, the next few days brought with it a still-distant God, and it seemed my fate as a remedial Christian was forever sealed.

My internal spiritual self-doubt worked its way to my face, and Fred could see my stress. He'd hoped I'd taken his words to heart and that I would see feeling distant from God as good thing. Instead, I felt like the inferior oddball, and I projected it onto him.

Over the next few days, if Fred offered just the slightest correction in my spiritual behavior or a tip on monastic etiquette, my self-pity turned to anger, and I'd launch into a rant. Had he forgotten that I was not a nun and that this was my first go at monastic living?

"Have you ever heard of fatback?" I had asked the monks as Fred drove the community members down the mountain thirty minutes to Hendy Woods, a Redwood park.

"Nope, never heard of it," they all replied, puzzled.

"It's a piece of animal lard that Southerners like to put into the pot of beans while they are cooking. It melts away and flavors the food."

Everyone was silent. And I was the only one who didn't notice it was awkward. Fred broached the topic later that day.

"Did you notice that the conversation stopped after you mentioned fatback?"

"No, it didn't."

"Yes, it did," he replied adamantly. "Dana, please don't talk about those kinds of things around the monks. You sounded like an old Southern grandmother reminiscing about her carnivorous days."

I grew hot with embarrassment. I only wanted them to know to ask if their beans were cooked in lard if they happened to be dining in the Bible Belt. The moment's pain turned to anger, and I replied in kind.

"Lighten up, Fred! They are humans."

"And another thing, I want you to hang your clothes out to dry on the line and be mindful of the energy you're consuming here." Fred was on a roll, and I was already mad, so he saw no harm in putting it all out there.

"Ugh. They have a dryer for a reason, Fred."

"And that dryer runs on solar power. And you shouldn't wash and dry a load of clothes each day—not like you do at home."

"But I feel dirty."

"You feel dirty thirty minutes after you shower. Deal with it."

Could Fred not see what a spiritual limb I was going out on even by being there—let alone watching my words and living austerely?

"Don't you see what a sacrifice I've made to come out here with you?" I asked.

Fred sighed, frustrated. "Dana, I want you to see this trip not as a sacrifice, but as an opportunity to serve, which will, in turn, benefit you."

Spoken like a true monk.

"I don't know any other wives who would vacation at a remote monastery when they could be lounging on the beach," I responded.

Fred walked out of the cabin to go see the cows, leaving me to sulk. His suggestions made me feel like an entitled princess with no sense of appropriate spiritual behavior. And maybe I was.

I sat by myself in our cabin, sobbing and blubbering. Why did I always forget that though God's love and attention flowed down on me, devotion and service must flow up too? It was a two-way street of relationship building I never seemed to have mastered, or, at the very least, made it through training wheels. But Gaudiya Vaishnavas serve God, unequivocally, unconditionally, and without concern for what God can do for them.

I was writing furiously in my journal when Fred returned. I'd calmed down and accepted his presence as a blessed reminder that our interfaith marriage kept me from being so stuck in my selfishness. Even in my pain I felt movement, and it was because my Hindu husband cared enough to show me the life that meant so much to him.

That afternoon, when my eyes were less puffy, I returned to the temple, this time with the intention of doing something special for God. I decided that God must like a clean house, so I pulled the mop from its nook and got to work.

As I mopped, I faced the deities I didn't yet understand and asked them to help me make God the center of my life. I hadn't had much faith that I'd get a response, but the answer came almost immediately. I reflected on how it came to pass that I was at a Hindu monastery, married to a former monk, and washing a temple floor. In that moment, God was in the center more than I'd noticed in a long time. The Gaura-Nitai deities were perfectly golden under the altar's lights, and I wondered if they heard my prayer. I mopped a little harder, with more elbow grease, like a diligent servant, in case God *was* watching.

The mop took me to the corner of the room I'd been avoiding all along, and I slowly inched toward Swami's empty chair. My face turned bright red when I remembered the summer afternoon I was so frustrated with Fred that I rammed our vacuum cleaner into the front leg of our living room altar. I felt calmer now, careful to guide the mop gingerly around Swami's chair while I inhaled the deities' mercy.

Had I married a Christian, warming the pews of a simple Baptist church and loving Jesus might have been easier. But then I wouldn't be here, learning the lessons of which I so desperately needed to be reminded. Had Fred and I not met, my faith journey may have stagnated into a comfortable lull of barely knowing Jesus and leaving God on the periphery of my life. The deities seemed infused by the Holy Spirit, and I remembered that it was a miracle to have this opportunity to merge Gaudiya Vaishnavism's practices into my own Christianity. For all this marriage's frustration, it was teaching us both how to better fulfill the greatest commandment: loving God.

The floor glistened in the afternoon light, Swami's chair was safe from my interfaith marriage wrath, and I slumped to my knees.

"Thank you, God," I said to the deities.

✝ ॐ ✝ ॐ ✝ ॐ ✝ ॐ ✝ ॐ ✝ ॐ ✝ ॐ ✝ ॐ ✝ ॐ ✝ ॐ ✝ ॐ ✝

Swami lives in the small upstairs room of the first structure built at Audarya. He generously offered us time to sit with him and talk about resolving our religious tensions.

Being in close proximity to Swami made my heart beat a little too quickly and my palms sweat. His spiritual advancement made me feel as if God lent him some omniscient powers, and mind reading must have been one of them. I just knew Swami could see right through me—straight to my heart, which had hardened with irrational jealousy and a Protestant heritage that questioned whether anyone but Jesus could tell me what to do.

"Remember, he jumps on trampolines," Fred said, squeezing my hand as we creaked up the narrow spiral staircase to Swami's room. Months before, Fred had shown me a photo of the saffron-clad Swami smiling and laughing while jumping on a trampoline in someone's backyard. In that frame, he was just like the rest of us, as human as bad hair days and spinach in our teeth.

But Swami wasn't on a trampoline that day. He was seated in a wooden rocking chair near the top of the stairs, and we each bowed our heads and pressed our chests to the floor in reverence before we took our spots before him. I was trying not to shake or hyperventilate.

After some small talk, Fred carefully broached the *guru*-disciple relationship as one of our relationship's deepest challenges. Swami nodded with understanding and responded in a way that was indicative of his Catholic youth—a boon to speaking a language that I understood.

"The Reformation was about throwing out the intermediary and offering a direct line to God," Swami proposed.

Exactly! I said in my mind and wondered if he were going to back me on this one.

"But the *guru*, properly understood, is not a detour to God. A *guru*'s knowledge and example is his or her spiritual authority. If we are truly interested in progress, we are happy to associate with this person. The ability to progress on one's own is limited. As hard as the Protestants have tried to get away from having *gurus*, they've failed."

Swami's words puzzled me until I realized that he was referring to the priests, pastors, and teachers that have shaped Protestant spirituality for centuries. My mind flashed through the slideshow of Martin Luther, John Calvin, Roger Williams, and John Wesley. These were men who influenced the entire trajectory of the church and its mainline Protestant denominations.

"The tendency is to get away from *gurus* because of failed or corrupted authority," Swami continued.

In Gaudiya Vaishnavism, much like many Eastern traditions, a *guru*-disciple relationship is required to advance on a spiritual path. Protestants have no such requirement, and Catholics have a variation of the Eastern principle through the local priest who works within the larger confines of the church. Baptists, fiercely independent creatures that we are, fear any spiritual authority that attempts to tell us what to do. But the solution, Swami explained, "Is not to do away with spiritual authority. You will still have it—but it doesn't need to be formalized. *Gurus* can be next-door neighbors whom you perceive to be 'walking the talk.' They are people who are further along and better equipped than you. And they enhance your progress."

Swami's words softened my autonomous shell, and the faces of the saints on my path came flooding forth. They were the faithful pilgrims of Binkley Baptist Church, First Baptist Church, Duke Divinity School, and my hospital chaplaincy. They'd led with their love and example—and helped me see my spiritual potential. Where would I be without them? Had my family, friends, and local church "*gurus*" not invested time, attention, and care with me, would I have even turned out to be a Christian? Would I have been ordained? How would I have moved forward?

Turns out, Protestants *still* have *gurus*, unbeknownst to them. But what about Hinduism's *gurus*, who, at first sight, appear to be self-appointed and holier that the rest of us because of the esteem in which their students hold them? Swami described the modern-day Hindu *guru* as God's grace—not a ploy for men and women to be worshiped and elevated above others.

"God cares for us enough to bestow mercy on us by showing us how best to serve. Grace has been bestowed on someone who is more advanced and who can now show us the way," Swami explained. "We shouldn't envy someone whom we perceive to be more advanced at living like Christ than we are. Instead, we should feel joy that God cares enough to send that person to show us what to do."

I hadn't thought about God appointing *gurus* to help us figure out this mess of a life. But that is exactly what Jesus was: the ultimate *guru* and the ultimate grace. And that's precisely what the hometown *gurus* I'd known—the dear followers of Jesus—had done for me.

A real *guru*, like Christ, will always point to God. The saints I'd known in my childhood and adolescence embodied God's grace—and accurately represented God by that grace. And I thought of the formal sense of *guru*, like the relationship between Swami and Fred, and how much Swami had helped Fred grow and stretch toward God. If Fred hadn't found Swami, would he be such a devout Hindu?

"God is so merciful that he sends someone to teach us personally how to serve. Mercy comes to us. This is the power of grace. Instead of thinking, 'There is a man there, and he is in the way,' you can transform that into 'God does this for us!' The *guru*," Swami explained, "then feels indebted to that mercy and grace and wants to share it with others."

Swami said that modern-day *gurus* can avoid pitfalls by saying, "I'm advanced *because* I'm living like Christ, but I'm only able to live like this because of God's mercy and strength."

The emotion in Swami's voice told me he was speaking from personal experience. Any spiritual authority he perceived in himself is shared by caring for and teaching students like Fred. The animosity toward spiritual authority I'd felt nearly all my life had been misplaced, but God extended me grace one more time—in the form of a holy man dressed in saffron robes who occasionally jumped on trampolines.

Just as we closed our discussion on the principle of the *guru*, and I was ready to leave and absorb everything the sage had taught us, Fred asked another question.

"Guru Maharaja, could you also talk about deity worship? Dana sometimes has a difficult time with it, as many Christians associate it with idolatry and the golden calf from the Old Testament."

I wanted to smack Fred on the back of the head. Instead, crimson crept up my neck and flushed my face with embarrassment. Had we not revealed enough of my Hindu suspicions for one day? My hesitations about the *guru* alone were enough to make me look less than open to Fred's spiritual path. But I did have lingering suspicions about the practice, as well as the time, money, and attention poured into deity worship when Hindu monks could hit the streets and feed God's children.

"Deity worship is a powerful practice that appears to run in contradiction to biblical teachings. But deity worship doesn't stem from an idea in the material mind. It is a well-founded system of worship described in Eastern scripture. It is not our imagination, and it's not for attaining anything material. Deity worship actually translates well to Christianity."

My ears perked up. How was that possible?

Then Swami recited a long list of Christianity's material objects that are, in most cases, considered sacred and worthy of worship by Protestants: the Bible, the cross, and Communion.

I remembered the Communion tables from my youth. Even in the most "low church" circumstances, all objects on the table—as well as the table itself—inspired reverence. I was taught at an early age that Communion tables were not made to hold purses, drinks, or people. Bibles were never to be placed on the floor or stepped on. And at Duke Divinity School, I learned the more orthodox practices of handling Eucharist and processing the gospel and cross. How many times had I seen professors reverently pick bread crumbs off the floor in the chapel? They didn't want anyone trampling Jesus. The devout Methodist and Episcopalian students would drink the reminder of the grape juice from the common cup after worship—or they poured it into the grass in the shape of a cross. Over time, even this Baptist had learned that these apparently ordinary objects had deep meaning for Christians, and they were to be handled with care.

Swami continued, "These materials objects become a junction between time and eternity. Time and space are the material elements—like a pen, paper, or cross—while eternity is the reality that one experiences by approaching these symbols at this junction."

Swami explained humanity's tendency to be captivated by shiny objects and pleasing smells. Prayer and chanting are beneficial spiritual practices, and each has its place, but deity worship engages the mind and senses in a way that meditation cannot. Drawing a parallel from deity wor-ship to Bibles, Communion, and crosses made the Hindu practice more relatable.

Although the principle of holy objects applies in both traditions, Gaudiya Vaishnavas have a more precise form of God described by scrip-ture, while Christians have an abstract idea of the Divine and rely on his-torical and cultural descriptions of Christ. For Hindus, vivid descriptions of God's form, qualities, and daily life are found in the Vedic scripture, which encourages them to craft and worship representations of God made out of material elements.

The deity, then, becomes a central focus of the community—the way the Bible is integral to the Christian tradition. Faith in the deity manifests itself in the daily schedule that revolves around the deities, their temple, gardens, and cows.

My joints ached from the hard floor, my heart hurt from all the truth, and I was ready to have some time alone to think and reflect on all the universal wisdom that Swami had offered. In just a few short hours, he had made meaningful connections between problems Fred and I had been muddling through for months.

And that's why he's the *guru*.

† ॐ † ॐ † ॐ † ॐ † ॐ † ॐ † ॐ † ॐ † ॐ † ॐ † ॐ † ॐ †

The next few days, I felt calmer, less tense, as if Swami's words had been the antidote I so desperately needed. I fell into the groove of the monastic rhythm, observing Fred and the monks as their days centered on the com-munity's most important task: serving God.

Running a monastery requires impeccable care and attention to deity worship, cooking, milking and caring for cows, maintaining facilities, planning and harvesting vegetable and flower gardens, all while receiving guests like me who sometimes mistakenly ask, "Can I have some of that (unoffered) milk in the refrigerator?"

Although a life of serving God and *guru* seems like it might be smooth sailing to an outsider, I quickly understood why this lifestyle was not for everyone. It is easy to think that monastic life is subdued, focused, and simple. But spending three meals per day with the monks was enough to tell me how physically, mentally, and emotionally rigorous a God-centered life was. The monks not only shared the bliss of a spirit-filled life—they also shared colds and exhaustion.

Even for the most spiritually balanced person, I can imagine that it would feel like the work is unending, the walls are closing in, and there is no breathing room to just be—to cry, throw a tantrum, or punch a pillow. Or maybe I was just projecting.

One night after worship, I said to Fred, "I can see why you left the monastery. It is really difficult to live this life."

"It was difficult for me, but some people are well-suited for it."

"It seems psychologically challenging—like being in a fishbowl. It's hard to have a bad day or to take time off to be melancholy because the entire community is counting on one another," I said, thinking of the service to be done, the shared meals, and worship hours.

"You have to be psychologically balanced to live this kind of life. I had a lot of imbalances when I lived here—which made it difficult for me, and I'm sure I made it difficult for others," Fred responded.

I continued, "And you have to work so hard. Waking up by 4:00 a.m. would make me sleep deprived. When do the monks get time for themselves or a weeklong vacation at the beach? I bet they get sick a lot."

And Fred, in his typical Eastern fashion, answered, "Swami is very accommodating, and if someone needs some time off, they just have to ask. Besides, many people outside the monastery work just as hard, maybe harder. But what are they working for? They are spending so much time and energy to maintain a life that will end at any moment."

"Hmmm. True," I admitted.

"I don't think anyone can avoid working hard. But the monks are investing all their energy into serving God. And that is a much better reason to be tired and worn out," he continued.

And ten days spent at a remote monastery tucked into the Redwoods of California with deities, a *guru*, and God was enough to make anyone realize that service to God and others is what makes for a full life.

† ॐ † ॐ † ॐ † ॐ † ॐ † ॐ † ॐ † ॐ † ॐ † ॐ † ॐ † ॐ †

Throughout our visit, I watched Fred's mood intensely—keeping alert for signs of regret or longing—as well as an eagerness to leave. But Fred seemed content with our arrangement: long days at Audarya devoted to service and study and a little relief of our relationship's pressure. I was grateful he hadn't tossed me or his wedding ring out the door.

At the monastery, Fred exhibited his typical spiritually idealistic self: contemplative, devout, and humbly reverent. I missed Fred's silliness, but he walked steadily through our Audarya days with more confidence and balance than he had described in his previous monastic tenure. There didn't seem to be a longing to return to this life, but instead, an overwhelming sense of calling to help the monks there because he knew what it felt like to be one of them. He confessed to me that he hoped any small role he could play would alleviate their load. Fred was *Gauravani* through and through: devoted, selfless, and focused on God—which was exactly what attracted me to him in the first place.

✝ ॐ ✝ ॐ ✝ ॐ ✝ ॐ ✝ ॐ ✝ ॐ ✝ ॐ ✝ ॐ ✝ ॐ ✝ ॐ ✝ ॐ ✝

Before Fred and I left the monastery, we asked Swami one more question: "What will make our interfaith marriage work?"

Swami smiled and thought for a moment.

"There will always be points of tension. What makes it work, though, is the unifying ideal that encourages you to rise above and make sacrifices. The religious relationship will be successful to the extent that the religious ideals are held above any other ideals.

"You both want the other to grow closer to God. It's important to honor the other person's faith and tradition above anything else. When you each do that, it works."

We would find balance if we *both* worked to put God in the center of our lives and honor the other partner's chosen path. But how do we continue to hold the other person's religious ideals above our own when they are so different?

"Identifying the unifying principles in each tradition is the closest way to getting to be in the 'same' religion," Swami answered.

I now had a glimpse of the *guru*'s nectar that Fred adored and the monastery that he loved but could not remain. I had been given a gift: a window to Fred's formation and the spiritual influences of his past. I was the fortunate spectator of his former life with all its strengths and vulnerabilities.

Fred knew Audarya would be transformational for us, just as India was. Ten days in a monastic community with *prasad*, prayer, and a heart-to-heart with Fred's *guru* softened my previously bitter attitude. I found myself grateful for Swami's wisdom and praying to the divinely infused Gaura-Nitai deities. I found myself loving the people and holy spaces that had turned Fred into who he is: a devout Hindu whose eagerness to always place God in the center was rubbing off on me.

In morning worship on the last day, while the monks' heads were bowed in quiet singing and reverence, Fred turned to me and whispered, "I love you."

It was an "I love you" I hadn't heard before. It came from his soul, and it was woven with "Thank you" and "I'm so glad you're here." It was alive and as full as the green treetops outside the temple walls.

Fred really did love me. He wasn't going to leave me for the monastic life he'd once had. He would return home with me, and we'd continue this wild ride of merging a Baptist's independent ways with a Hindu's God-focused simplicity.

Now, I could see clearly that most of our bickering was pointless and that my agreeing to come to Audarya, no matter the motives or spiritual immaturity, meant more to him than anything I could say or do.

We said our good-byes on a warm Thursday morning, when the community rhythm was only temporarily interrupted with heartfelt hugs and thanks. We were returning to the "real" world—a difficult transition after being suspended in ten days of divinity, dipped in the grace and hospitality that is communal living. We were so well cared for that I felt a little guilty. I only hoped, that, despite my emotional rollercoaster, I had provided some service while we were there.

AUDARYA

We arrived home a different couple than when we left. The bickering was squelched, and I was convinced that we'd been given a precious gift of interfaith marriage.

For all the chaos, darkness, and disagreements, the treasure of this Christian-Hindu partnership is an enriched spiritual path for Fred and me. And it seems to me that this is grace: God is merciful enough to show up in many forms and many circumstances. We see God by the renewal and love we experience. This is how we are sure we've been in the presence of the Divine, even if that presence looks different from what we are used to.

Shortly after we returned home, Fred and I knelt together before our altar—the one that has both Jesus Christ and Hindu deities, a *guru*, and scripture from each tradition. We thanked them all for the respite we'd just experienced and for the many ways in which the Holy is revealed. When we agree to clothe ourselves with love and meet in that common space where God is at the center, we know we will succeed.

CHAPTER

MIRRORS

For now we see in a mirror, dimly. . . . Now I know only in part;
then I will know fully, even as I have been fully known. And now faith, hope,
and love abide, these three; and the greatest of these is love.

1 Corinthians 13:12-13, NRSV

I visited the Hindu temple on what felt like the coldest day of Lent. Yearning for God and feeling Binkley's thirty-minute distance, I opted for the nearby Sri Venkateshwara Temple where Fred and I attend. The temple, expansive and ornate, is lovingly referred to by the locals as "Balaji Temple." It sits off a busy road but is hidden from commuters and day-to-day traffic. Halfway down the drive, a brilliant white stone façade is exposed from behind the trees, decadent with the architecture of South Indian temples. Inside, gray-black marble floors are cool beneath pilgrims' feet and large pillars set a mood of reverence.

It was just before noon when I arrived by myself, immediately transported back to an India-like sacred escape amid a bustling life. There were no other visitors inside, save for an elderly Indian gentleman speaking with the priest who must have been ten years his junior. The Indian priest was bare-chested and wore a saffron *dhoti*, a long piece of cloth draped to make men's pants. The two of them chatted softly in a language I did not recognize, melodic syllables dancing between them.

This was only the second time I'd visited the temple by myself, but I knew the liturgical moves from four years of watching Fred. He'd shown me the points in the room at which I should lower myself to my hands and knees with my head bowed to the floor in obeisance. When Fred worships here, he lies prostrate on the floor in utter humility, similar to what I'd seen Catholic and Episcopal ordinands do.

Much like Audarya, Sri Venkateshwara's large temple room is segmented by a sanctum sanctorum that holds its most prominent deity: Sri Vishnu, or here known as Balaji. Balaji's room is large enough for foot traffic, so devotees enter in to take *darshan*. The hope is that you will see God, and, ultimately, God will see you. I swept my hand over the threshold as I entered the room, gathering the dust of faithful pilgrims who had passed before me.

Two *ghee* lamps illumined God's form as a four-armed giant adorned with brass accoutrements. His room smelled of incense, sandalwood, and ancient places. Sri Vaishnavism is Gaudiya Vaishnavism's high church cousin. Sri Vishnu evokes a Catholic-like mood of awe and reverence, while Gaudiya Vaishnavism feels intimate and sweet, like a Jesus-loving Baptist service. Sri Vaishnavas consider Vishnu to be the Supreme Personality of God, while Gaudiya Vaishnavas deem it to be Krishna. The two sects get along in spite of this minor detail because at the end of the day, they agree that both Vishnu and Krishna are God.

I paused to pray before Balaji in the dim light, my hands pressed together at my chest. I asked God to walk with me this Lent, when things are dark and cold and it's easy to feel like the sun—or Jesus—will never rise again.

"Give me hope, Lord," I prayed. "Easter hope," I added for good measure, just so we were clear.

I moved to the right side of the room to receive a blessing from the priest, who had paused his conversation to offer his sacramental duty.

"*Hare Krishna!*" the priest said in a high-pitched and animated voice, the way only Indians can speak it. His greeting meant that he knew I was not a Sri Vaishnava. My pale skin and the *japa* bead bag that hung around my neck had given me away. It was the same bead bag that pressed on my heart in India, the one that held Fred's first set of prayer beads.

"*Hare Krishna*," I whispered back, shyly.

I'd brought the bead bag as insurance, should anyone suspect I was a journalist or an evangelical Christian ready to spray-paint slanderous messages on the walls that all Hindus were going to hell. Wearing it meant that I knew a little something about Hinduism and that I was there to worship, not cause trouble.

"How are you?" he asked, which was highly unusual for a Sri Vaishnava priest. Most of them are somber and quintessentially monastic, avoiding small talk and eye contact.

I mumbled something inaudible, bashful from this unexpected friendliness. Instead, my body moved with muscle memory of Eucharist: back curved humbly, hands out, knowing that none of us really deserves the grace that is being offered. I held my cupped right hand up to accept water he was prepared to spoon into my palm, the camphor-infused liquid that had been offered to Balaji and was now *prasad*.

I pressed my hand to my lips and sipped the holy water, just as I would the cup of the New Covenant in Jesus Christ. Once the water was gone, I glided my hand over my forehead and down the back of my head the way I'd seen all the Hindus do, careful not to let any drop hit the floor or be wasted.

I pressed my palms together to my chest and bowed my head in preparation for the next blessing, what I call "the helmet." This medieval-looking contraption is a brass hat that the priest momentarily places over your head. Turns out that it is an actual helmet belonging to Balaji, and I wondered if the Christian church would have had an equivalent ritual had Jesus worn a head covering.

"Thank you," I whispered, feeling badly about my previous socially awkward responses to his unusual priestly friendliness.

I scooted out of the sanctum sanctorum in a stiff backward shuffle, without turning my back on the Lord, just as Fred had taught me. I took a seat at the back of the large temple room, pressed against the black marble where I could still see Balaji and the altar. In the gray of noonday March,

I wrote pages of prayers while the cool floor transported me back to the predawn mornings of my Indian honeymoon.

Thirty minutes later, the temple pace picked up, and Indian visitors came and went, bustling in during their lunch hours. The priest stood at his station in the sanctum sanctorum, blessing all who entered for *darshan*. He chanted quickly between pilgrims, the hum of his words escaping from the small space and reverberating into the temple room.

I could have made the trek that day to Binkley, but it felt too distant, and I needed God now—this minute—to fill the emptiness of Lenten drudge that comes with working hard at being contemplative. I came to the Hindu temple because I knew that God was just as present here as in Baptist sanctuaries and Catholic cathedrals. Beautiful, expansive God was mercifully showing up as Jesus, Spirit, Vishnu, and Krishna.

The season of Lent made me consider the journey that brought me to this place. I'd been formed by two loving Baptist communities, a United Methodist seminary, and a hospital; ordained as a Southern Baptist minister at twenty-one; and renewed by the faith of a Hindu husband. I'd found my way to the temple that Wednesday because I knew Jesus was there, with Vishnu and Krishna, embodied in *darshan, prasad,* and in the hospitable welcome of a kind priest.

In just four short years of knowing Fred, I was just as sure of Christ's birth, ministry, death, and resurrection as ever. I found Jesus in our vegetarianism, our interfaith sabbath-keeping, and our discussions of Christian-Hindu differences. Along the way, I discovered that God—my God—was just as real in the opulent form of Balaji, illumined by the light of *ghee* lamps, as in the familiar spaces of Binkley Baptist Church and First Baptist Church.

I prayed for forty-five minutes, scribbling down wonderings of Jesus' inclusive ministry and his rejection of keeping things the way they'd always been. What would Jesus have said about our Christian-Hindu marriage? I imagine he'd approve, because it goes against the status quo.

"Thank you, Jesus," I whispered, "for sending a Hindu to draw me closer to you."

I got up and walked to the temple's back door, where the priests kept a large stainless steel pot of rice and *dahl* on a kindergarten table. The pot was always here, full and steaming, the Ayurvedic version of loaves and fishes. It was *prasad,* the consecrated holy food and form of radical hospitality that warmed my social justice heart. It was the culinary version of the neon sign all faith communities should place on their doors: *Come in, you hungry and lonely of the world. Come to the House of the Lord and be fed!* This is Communion, every day, all day—a perfect way to live faith.

I scooped myself a little *prasad* and placed it on the red and white checked napkins the priests kept on the table. The priest was on break from distributing blessings, walking through the large temple room, energized by the lunchtime infusion of people.

I pushed open the heavy wooden door to the outside, balancing my *prasad* in one hand and my notebook in the other. With the door halfway open, I looked back to catch the priest's attention to offer a smile of gratitude. He saw me and waved, and as I waved back, I overturned my napkin of *prasad.* The rice landed with a splat on the concrete. My face flushed, and I stepped outside, pushing the door to the temple room closed as quickly as I could, praying he hadn't noticed I'd just dumped the equivalent of Holy Communion on the dirty stone steps.

I breathed a quick prayer of petition to help me figure out what I should do. The Hindu version of Jesus' broken body was slathered there, in a not-so-appetizing way.

And then a miracle occurred. Without thinking, my knees bent my body down to the ground, and my fingers gathered every cubic inch of *prasad* up from the place where everyone's feet step out of the temple. Me, absence of toilet-paper fearing, allergic-to-dirt-and-chaos Dana, who *hated* dusty feet and eating with her hands, picked up rice that had been on the ground far longer than five seconds. And then—I ate it! There, in the Lenten daylight on the steps of a Hindu temple, I shoved what was likely subject to foot fungi and God-knows-what-else in my mouth—joyfully. I ate *prasad* right off the ground, without hesitation.

This felt like metaphor for my new interfaith life. I was no longer bothered by the chaos that came from blurring east-meets-west frameworks. Interfaith living was sometimes a crazy-making struggle, and sometimes Jesus and God and Krishna were pushed to the background while Fred and I kept our sanity. But the dirt and shadows that some claimed to be the dangers of being an interfaith couple were not valid. A Christian-Hindu life is messy—like *prasad* dropped on the concrete—but I cherish it. Spilling our overflowing cup was an honor, not a trouble. No matter how off track Fred and I felt our interfaith marriage was at times, God was still God, and we were still seeking the Divine, incarnate in many forms.

Four years ago, I would have tossed the Communion in the trash can without thinking because it had fallen on the ground. Now, I ate it heartily because I understood what the early Christian community experienced as evidenced in the Gospel of John: Jesus is the Bread of Life—even if sometimes that bread is rice served at a Hindu temple.

As Christians, we may think we've cornered the market on God. We cling to our religious traditions as the only true way to spiritual enlightenment or eternal life. Our convictions run deep, influencing how we move about the world and treat one another. When we feel threatened, we oppress and condemn others' journeys with our scripture and dogma. The human need for calming chaos makes us place God in a little box with sharp edges and straight lines. Our biggest fear is that when we open ourselves to others' understanding of God, we will jeopardize our own path. And yet, the opposite is true. The Holy Spirit breaks free from our human-made constraints and moves fluidly among us, crossing our unnecessary lines drawn in the sand.

Spiritual growth happens when we challenge ourselves to sincere dialogue with someone for whom God looks very different. Interfaith conversations hold mirrors to our own beliefs, where we see both brightness and room for transformation. Fred's Hinduism has reformed my Christian life. He's shown me an Eastern fulfillment and freedom that comes with getting rid of the actual and proverbial clutter. Now I'm more apt to focus on a faith integrated with life that cultivates a deeper relationship with Jesus. My "What have you done for me lately, God?" has morphed into, "Show me how to serve you, Jesus."

Before meeting my former Hindu monk, I tricked myself into believing that achievements and acquisitions were the true stuff of life. I neglected my true nature as a spark of Divine energy that should reflect the grace I had been given. But Fred reminded me of this duty when he graciously shared his beliefs and discoveries with me.

Fred learned in a few short years what most of us never figure out in a lifetime: we are all holy creatures whose true happiness lies in prioritizing our relationship with God. While I was content with a call-on-God-in-need arrangement, Fred understood that the powerful interaction we crave can only come when we integrate the Holy into every aspect of our lives.

It feels like only yesterday that I checked eHarmony boxes in my pajamas, bossing God around about what I would and would not accept in a partner. Now I'm married to a former Hindu monk, so the joke's on me. I dove, baptism-by-fire style, into an integrated Christian-Hindu life. I visited physical and metaphorical spaces of pain and change: an Indian honeymoon, a fledgling sabbath routine, dietary challenges, dark days of disagreements, and ten days in a remote monastery.

Soulmates are the partners and friends who show us who we really are. They hold mirrors to our hearts, reflecting what makes us real and lovable, while also shedding light on the bruised and callused spots that need work. They encourage us to live into our most precious calling: becoming the spiritual creatures we are meant to be.

Fred held up a mirror that reflected a life formed by supportive church and academic communities, a loving family, and many friends. But it also reflected a young woman whose faith had shriveled to one-hour sabbaths and a dying curiosity for the Sacred. I had become apathetic toward my own spiritual growth; I wasn't reading or talking about God, or even living in a way that indicated Jesus was important in my life.

My Hindu partner helped me make over my life in a way that looks and feels more like the one I was called to on that Sunday when I told God and everyone else, "Here I am, Lord. Send me."

Fred gave me the greatest gift this side of heaven: a Hinduism that brought me back to Jesus.